PRIDE AND PASSION IN
BURY
A LANCASHIRE BIOGRAPHY

PRIDE AND PASSION IN

BURY

A LANCASHIRE BIOGRAPHY

EAMON KAVANAGH

DB
PUBLISHING

First published in Great Britain in 2012 by Derby Books Publishing Company Ltd, 3 The Parker Centre, Mansfield Rd, Derby, DE21 4SZ

ISBN 978-1-78091-162-5

Contents

The Letter

The peaceful atmosphere of class 4-b's English lesson was interrupted by a barely audible knock at our classroom door. After our class teacher, Mr. Tonges' command to enter, the door slowly opened and in walked little Helen Brown from the first year. Helen timidly made her way to where the class teacher stood. All eyes fixed on Helen. The words she then uttered certainly heightened my attention. "I've been asked to give this to Eamon Kavanagh." At that moment, fear and excitement battled for dominance in my adrenaline flooded body. In Helen's hand, she held an envelope, its contents as yet unknown to me. Mr. Tonge motioned to me to make my way to where he and Helen stood. In my confused state, I made my way to Helen. After taking the envelope from her outstretched hand and thanking her, I stood there impersonating a dummy, awaiting instruction from my teacher as to what to do next. Indecision reigned for maybe a second or two but with the whole of the class's attention fixed on me, it felt a whole lot longer. Mr. Tonge informed me I may read the letter as it "may be important." After extracting the letter from the envelope, these words unfolded before my eyes:

5.9.1969
27 Royal Avenue,
Bury.

Dear Sir,

I am writing on behalf of Manchester City F.C. regarding your son Eamon. I have seen him playing previously and am quite sure with luck and the ability he shows he could do well. I would be obliged if I could call to see you regarding Eamon being trained and coached by my club.

If possible I would appreciate a conversation on Sunday 7.9.1969 regarding schoolboy forms and any other questions you require.

Yours in anticipation,
B. Walker

After reading the letter, my breathing was so erratic it rendered my young self incoherent. In answer to Mr. Tonge's worried expression, I passed him the letter to read for himself. After doing so, along with my agreeing nod, he proceeded to read the wonderful words to the expectant boys and girls. Our teacher had barely began reading but as the words "Manchester City F.C." left his lips, pandemonium ensued, my male classmates were all over me, backslapping and handshakes from each in turn, the girls for there part were chanting my name. As the commotion was attracting attention from the occupants of the next door classroom, Mr. Tonge had no option but to regain order. As things began to settle down and everyone, bar myself, returned to their seats, Mr. Tonge turned to me and said, "Eamon, I think it's best if you make your way home now. I can safely say your concentration level will be compromised. Will there be anyone at home?" Yes! "Well you get yourself home with the good news and I'll see you again on Monday."

My wave goodbye to my classmates was answered by a rapturous clapping, adding to my emotional state. After passing through the school gates, thoughts shooting through my overloaded mind and my body pulsing adrenaline, I was left with no option but to run, and run fast. If not I would surely burst. So off I set, trying to navigate safely while fabulous thoughts invaded my mind. Me, Eamon Kavanagh, running out onto the pristine Maine Road pitch, along with my City team mates, to thunderous applause, strange, unedited noises emitting from my throat. As I approached the running track on Wellington Road, I brushed aside the shouts of a couple of mates to join them for a kick about (obviously "wagging" school). Had they no sense of occasion?

I arrived at the front door of my home, dripping with sweat and breathing heavily. I pushed the door open (it was never locked) and I found mum in the kitchen preparing our evening meal. I quickly put my worried looking mum at ease. "Relax mum, nothing's wrong, I'm home early for a good reason." I passed my mum the letter then just stood back and watched her face. I don't know what I was expecting but definitely not the tears that then filled her eyes, my introduction to tears of joy. We ended up hugging then mum made a brew. Mum carried on preparing our meal with me following her around, brew in hand, unable to settle, passing the afternoon in high spirits, awaiting the arrival of the rest of our family. "Roll on Sunday!"

Brian Walker proved to be a lovely fella. Thinking back it must have been a little daunting for Brian to enter the Kavanagh household with a full complement comprising Mum Teresa, Dad Patrick, and us eight kids. After accepting the customary cup of tea that was offered, there then ensued a good hour's chat, mainly Mum and Brian, Dad being a man of few words, unusual for an Irishman. The parting advice Brian left with Mum was "feed him plenty of steak, build him up" and then laughing "no women!" As young as I was, the relevance of his comment about me being fed steak wasn't lost on me. Mum and Dad worked hard but I knew money was tight. The thought of me sitting down with a huge steak on my plate and Dad looking enviously at my expensive succulent feast, paid for by the sweat of his brow, didn't fare well. Thinking back to the early years, I can't remember going without much. The luxuries were out but the things to keep body and soul together were always there.

Love Affair

As to the start of my love affair with the beautiful game, it almost certainly began with my older brother Pat purchasing a plastic Frido ball. Asking me out front for a 'kick about' his enthusiasm was infectious. The next two hours would be spent passing the ball between the two of us with occasional words of advice from Pat. Even at my tender age I realised I felt very comfortable with the ball at my feet. I knew then this was a game I would come to love.

After our Pat's "that'll do for today lad" we retired to the comfort of our three-bedroom council house in Goldfinch Drive (Dicky Bird estate), in the old mill town of Bury, nestled in the shadow of the Pennines in Lancashire. We were a close family, we had to be, as there were 10 of us. General harmony proved a necessity. We weren't the biggest family on the street, the Holts up the road had 14. In those days big families weren't unusual, especially in Irish Catholic families. I loved Dicky Bird Estate, for a young kid growing up it wasn't far from perfect.

The Games we Played

I'd sit on my wooden perch that separated us from next door, either waiting for another kid to play with or going in search of a playmate. The street out front at that time was free from cars. There were large back gardens, spare ground, beyond that Sid's field; Sid being the local farmer. A scary character indeed, rumour had it that if he caught you on his land he'd take you back to the farmyard where he had a couple of wooden posts. He would then tether the unruly kids to the posts in a hugging fashion. Their pants would then be pulled down. As they stood shaking and probably crying, Sid would proceed to fill his old shotgun with rock salt, then retired to a distance he knew would not cause too much damage, just enough for the salt to end up imbedded in the poor soul's bottom. On hearing this tale, true or false, there's no way Sid would ever catch me. Our paths would cross later in an incident I still don't quite understand, but enough for now.

There were woods nearby where me and a few pals would climb the trees and play 'Split the Kipper', a game involving two lads facing one another, both holding penknives. One lad would throw his knife within a few feet of his opponent; providing the knife was embedded blade first his opponent had to spread his legs to accommodate where the knife had landed. The second throw of the knife, to be successful, had to land between the outstretched legs. The danger would come when you were in a position of practically doing the splits and left praying your opponent was very deft with his knife.

On the spare ground at the back of Goldfinch Drive, along with a large Accrington brick air raid shelter were the remnants of a number of disused allotments whose forsaken produce was still quite abundant; rhubarb, carrots and spuds. During the long summer holidays our young imaginations would run wild. The girls, including my mate Billy Mottershead's sister Angela would organise us into small groups performing different circus-like feats, with a good fire going, using the wood we'd gathered, including an assortment of the vegetables cooking on said fire. Bravery was tested by entering the pitch black air raid shelter and the length of time spent in its terrifying bowels.

Another pastime was den making. I once set to work on my own den with real vigour, spending the best part of the afternoon erecting it, apart from a couple of visits home for some ornaments and essentials that I thought my mum wouldn't miss, that would give my den that homely look. The morning after my den's completion I sleepily came down our stairs wearing the statutory vest and only the vest. Pyjamas were a much later addition to Kavanagh males. Halfway down the stairs I looked up to meet the eyes of Billy's sister, Angela. No words passed between us, just a sad groan from me as I quickly about-turned, giving Angela full view of my boyish pride and joy. As I closed my bedroom door, muttering incoherent noises, I stopped, listened and heard Angela and the rest of my family fall into uncontrollable laughter. I later found out Angela had called round to see if our Kathleen was playing out. Lesson learned.

Three weeks later when I finally ventured out I took great care to make sure I avoided the lovely Angela. Things gradually got back to normal. Me and whoever was around at the time, after telling Mum we'd be back for tea, set out on excursions that would see us travel miles; Holcombe Hill, Bluebell Woods, the Lido or up to the water-filled quarries of Birtle. I consider this the saddest loss for kids today, the freedom we took for granted and simple pastimes we so enjoyed.

First Footy Boots

Life was simple and lovely. Things at my school, "St. Joseph's", had taken a turn for the better. I'd made the football team along with my mucker Paddy Holmes. The only cloud on the horizon being the fact I had no footy boots. I remember telling Mum I'd been selected for the school team and would need football boots. I knew money was short. Dad's wages navvying wouldn't stretch too far. My prayers were answered by my mate Billy Mottershead down the street. Billy said my Mum could buy his boots for a shilling. The fact that Billy's boots were three sizes too big and had three studs missing didn't dim my excitement and when Dad came home with 12 new leather studs, and watching him hammer each stud into the thick sole of my new boots, which came halfway up my ankles, I could hardly contain myself. The day finally came when as Captain I lead out my team, heroes every one of them. With our kit, green and white hooped shirts, white shorts and white socks we resembled a miniature Glasgow Celtic. I can't tell you how good I felt. We were playing St. Chad's who looked for all the world to me like giants. My nerves were jangling as the referee called me and the opposing captain together.

After shaking hands with the ref and their captain, I won the toss. As there was a slight slope, I opted to kick downhill. I couldn't help noticing their captain kept looking at my boots and smiling. Looking down, I understood the cause of his amusement, with my oversize boots, padded out with three pairs of woolly socks, I looked to all the world like Charlie Cairoli. As I looked up and met his gaze he burst out laughing. Fighting back tears, I could feel the blood rushing to my face. At that moment I just wanted the game to start.

Fifteen minutes into the game I hadn't touched the ball. I honestly think I was too embarrassed. Then, to add insult to injury, St. Chad's scored and guess who the scorer was? Yes, my tormentor who came running past me, laughing, accidently knocking my shoulder with his. This would be the defining moment where I would realise controlled anger could prove a real asset. On my next encounter with the ball, received on my favoured right wing, I set off on a run that would see me in their six yard box. After leaving three defenders floundering, I then unleashed a shot which took their 'keeper and the size four caseball into the back of the net. Before the end of the match I was to repeat this feat twice more. On completing my hat trick, I walked past their captain, winked and said "wanna buy em?"

Cumbersome my boots may have been, but toe bungs from reinforced leather-toed boots took some stopping. I knew then I would always be a winger. Fleet of foot, agile enough to change direction quickly, words would not suffice to describe my feeling on receiving a ball on the wing facing an opponent, I instinctively knew he'd have little chance of preventing me achieving my goal of reaching the dead ball line and putting a cross in, or all too often, assuming I could take their whole team on, finally losing the ball, then enduring shouts of "pass the ball you greedy git". Alas it was a long learning curve.

Boxing Day Joy

Playing with the bigger lads would stand me in good stead for the testing years to come. Our Pat had decided I was ready for my baptism to our own theatre of dreams, the Shakers of Gigg Lane fame. For my first professional football match our Pat's choice was Bury F.C. v Bolton Wanderers. I don't know what I was expecting but it didn't include me ending up on our Pat's shoulders just so I could breath easier. I've never seen a crowd like that at Gigg Lane and I doubt I ever will again.

The game finished one apiece and I really enjoyed it apart from fighting our way in and then fighting our way out. Pat's second choice, this time in the company of my younger brother Michael, was a day never to be forgotten. It was Boxing Day and Bury F.C. were playing away to Southport. The day unfolded as you'd expect, apart from yours truly being sick on the coach on our way there, much to the annoyance of our Pat. We got to the match safely and what a match, Bury running out 1–4 winners, Greg Farrell notching a couple of crackers. My memory won't release the other scorers.

At the final whistle three happy Kavanaghs made their way to the exits, reaching what we assumed to be the allotted pick-up spot for our coach, we waited and waited. Finally our Pat rushed me and Michael back to the ground. Pat must have looked a worried man. So much so that a lady passing enquired if he was alright. After listening to his tale of woe she patted Pat's shoulder and said "wait here."

The next thing we knew we were boarding the Bury team coach. Pat was a nervous wreck as we took our seats, smiling like Cheshire cats as we passed our heroes. Pat and Michael sat together and I sat by myself immediately behind them. Pat's first action after he sat down was to pop his head round and threaten me with bodily harm if I even looked like being sick.

When things quietened down I looked guardedly around at men I was in awe of. My boyhood hero and fellow Dicky Birdian Alec Lindsey, the fiery Scot Bobby Collins, the maestro himself Jimmy Kerr, the hero of the day, Greg Farrell. And Mr. Reliable, and, after a stop at a roadside pub, Mr. Generous, Brian Turner, who ruffled mine and Michael's hair and bought us pop and crisps. In later years Brian would open the Rosamar Café in Bury's precinct which was well patronised by the good folk of Bury. We owe that special day to that lovely lady, whoever she was.

The Airgun Bug

A time would come when I would be introduced to something that would take up money and many hours of my life. One afternoon our next-door neighbour Mick O' Reilly asked me if I'd like to join him in a little target practice with his air rifle, in his back garden. As Mick was a good bit older than me, Mum gave the go-ahead. Mick had placed a tin can in the solitary apple tree in the middle of his garden. After Mick had gone through the necessities with me, I took the rifle, raised it to eye-level, took aim and squeezed the trigger. The can was sent flying in the air and I was hooked.

In the following years I would spend many hours after setting out, with my rifle in a bag slung over my shoulder, ferret up my jumper, dog at my side, making my way along the banks of Bury's two main rivers, the Roach and the Irwell, following the old tradition of ratting. Anyway, thanks Mick!

As for the footy, the street games on Goldfinch were brilliant with up to 30 kids playing, half the time kids didn't bother with which side they were on, the way they were facing was good enough! The only problem being the ball. They were used so much on the concrete streets they were forever bursting. Occasionally, one of the kids did manage to block the hole with a red hot poker, but more often than not, it didn't work and no-one had enough money for a new one. At these times, desperate for a game, we'd make the short trip to the local Hoyles playing field; this was where the bigger lads tended to play their games, often with a proper lace up caseball. A few of us were allowed to play among them.

This would be where important lessons were learned. Dicky Bird had a lot of football talent. Names come to mind; Paul Lomax, the Skinner brothers and Alec Lindsey who went on to pro football with Bury F.C and Liverpool F.C. If there was no-one down with a ball, which was rare, we'd make our way back to Goldfinch and get a game of 'Kick the Can', 'Hide and Seek' or, my favourite, 'Kiss Catch' going. Obviously as autumn beckoned our enjoyable games petered out. Winter restricted us to customary winter pastimes, restricted by cumbersome, warm clothing.

New Best Mate

We enjoyed the snow that would reach drifts of several feet, having to make periodic trips home to warm frozen hands and feet. After tea we would accumulate outside for our last play of the day. The light would be fading before we made the short distance from school to Goldfinch. During one of these trips home me and my sister Kath were surprised to see a large lorry parked outside next door. Kath made her way through our front door, I, on the other hand, was curious to see who'd acquired our newly vacant house next door, Mick O' Reilly and his mother having vacated the property a couple of weeks before. Among the fellows humping the stuff inside, was a tall, skinny guy around my age. After agreeing to me giving him a hand, the next hour or so were spent emptying the lorry of all its contents, after which me and my new neighbour had time for a quick chat. His name was Mick Mahon. His family consisted of Mum, Dad and seven kids. After our chat my parting words were: "Wanna be my best mate?" His reply: "why not?"

What was I saying about a simple life? Turns out the Mahons were great neighbours. Even when Dad, after erecting a coat stand with screws so long their last 1/2 inch were left protruding through the Mahon's hallway. Dad's crack that they could hang their coats on the screws didn't go down too well!

Mum, at this time worked nights at Robinson Kay Home on Walmersley Road. On certain nights, with Dad gone for a drink, us younger kids were left in the care of our older siblings. All was well until one night they decided to have a séance using an Ouija board, already banned by the Catholic Church. Us younger kids were awakened from our slumber by the combined screams of our older brothers and sisters. The sight of our seniors almost hysterical had a terrible effect on us young ones. Myself, Margaret, Kathleen and baby Michael clung to one another for comfort. Order was only regained when Mrs. Mahon from next door, alarmed by the commotion, finally calmed the older ones down. The next morning Mrs. Mahon caught Mum at the front door, informing her of the night before's proceedings. All hell broke loose on finding the cause of the former night's unrest, Mum being a strong church-goer. One of the things Mum screamed out to my older brothers and sisters stuck with me. "Have you any idea what you could be fetching into the house?" This comment certainly gave me cause for concern.

It turned out, during said séance, a glass being used as a marker apparently rose off the table and smashed against the wall, thus creating pandemonium. Each member of the offending group was soundly tanned by Mum. I knew from experience how they were feeling towards Mum but their bitterness would soon disappear, they knew she would reassure each one of them during the day of her love for them.

Which brings me back nicely to the incident involving Mum which still has me a little confused. It started one summer's afternoon during the big holidays. There was a small graveyard at the lower end of Goldfinch just the other side of Chaffinch Drive. To get to it meant scaling a 6ft gate. Sid's field was on the other side. All that was left was a short stride to the right over a low wall. The reason for the effort in the first place was that myself, Billy and Mick had erected a rope swing over the outstretched branch of a big sycamore, providing us with great fun.

On the day in question, as the other lads were occupied indoors, I made the short journey myself. I'd only been impersonating Tarzan for a matter of minutes when, as I made the backward swing towards the cemetery wall, I was grabbed by the hair and forced to the ground while being continually punched and kicked. My first encounter with unprovoked aggression left me in a bit of a state. Not too much of a state that I wasn't able to peer over the cemetery wall and watch as my aggressor made his way home to the farmhouse. I was shocked to see and hear the laughing figure of one of Sid's young farmhands, Danny. Only once before had I seen him at close quarters, the year before helping Sid repair some damaged fencing in the bottom field. On returning home, given my Mum's reaction, my bruised face told its own story.

After informing her of what took place, Mum went on one. "What? That bully! He'd make two of you! Come on!" I was then led, half-running, half being dragged clean through the middle of Sid's field. A quick glance at Mum's face told me to forget any protests. We arrived at the door of the farmhouse where Mum's clenched-fist knock left no one in any doubt that she meant business. On answering the door, even grumpy old Sid immediately agreed with her order of "get him out here!" On stepping out into the yard, Danny and myself were pulled together by Mum, who then said loudly "now while I'm here." There then ensued a two-minute battle where, despite my new determination, I was again battered senseless. After a torrent of parting niceties, I was taken by the hand and more or less taken back the same way I was fetched with Mum mumbling things to herself I couldn't understand. That night I was sat down to a lovely tea, a bit worse for wear, staring lovingly into Mum's eyes then as now, wondering why?

Puppy Love

Whilst being of tender years, my young mind when not on football was tending on a very regular basis being spent thinking of how lovely one of my classmates, Maureen Bridge, was and how I could impress her. One day just before home time it came to me. How to win her affections. This was how it went: knowing where Maureen lived – the Crescent – the last part of her journey home took her down the back of Bell Lane, very quiet. My plan was, after tailing her to this area I would take off my gabardine mac. After pulling it over my shoulders I'd then fasten only the top button, thus forming a cape. It was now time for my Batman impression. From a position about 20 yards behind her I would break into a trot and then a gallop. As I passed Maureen at quite some speed, not saying anything, cape floating horizontally behind me like a super hero.

Yes, I know. What must have been going through the poor girl's head? At the height of my lovelorn efforts I'd be performing this worrying feat five days a week. It got me nowhere. On a couple of occasions I hid and watched as she reached her door, after a worried look around the door would slam and I'm sure I heard a bolt sliding shut.

Original St. Joseph's

My initial learning years were spent at the old St. Josephs Junior School on Peter Street, while waiting for the completion of the new school on Danesmoor Drive. Most events from that time are now a little vague. Certain memories, however, are still clear, like on cold days the small bottles of warm milk we so enjoyed and running round the yard like a lunatic just like all the other kids, excited over nothing more than being alive. My memories of the school itself are shady but I remember the interior being on the gloomy side, dark teak coloured furnishings. The small desks with their white pot ink wells and a small polished plank of wood for our little bottoms to gradually lose all feeling.

And one other thing I remember. The school was on Peter Street and when dinner time came round I remember Mrs. Hart, our Deputy Head Teacher, arranging us in single file. We would then be led around 60 yards further down Peter Street to a building on the same side as the school and church. We then climbed a couple of flights of stairs. I remember a huge room with tables arranged in an orderly fashion. After finishing my dinner I scanned the windows for the spy bird my Mum told me would always let her know if I hadn't eaten all my dinner. Mr. Colligan our headmaster was a larger than life, jolly fella. When, on rare occasions, I pass what was the schoolyard, the scene of us kids chasing each other and laughing at anything, and Christmas time, standing shoulder to shoulder singing beautiful hymns like "Once in Royal David's City" and my favourite, "Noel" slip easily into my mind as welcome memories.

First Irish Trip

To say we were surprised to be informed by mum and dad we were to take a trip across the Irish Sea was an understatement. People like us didn't go on holiday. They explained dad's parents weren't in great health. The trip would be financed from the compensation dad received from work after taking the end off his thumb after a pile of concrete slabs overbalanced. A week later we were boarding the boat at Hollyhead. The boat appeared old but sturdy. I found myself whispering a quiet prayer for a safe voyage. The boat would be battered by inclement weather. The effect on my 10 year old self was instant. The contents of my stomach being ejected soon after we left port, a small portion of which ended up in Dad's jacket pocket.

After cleaning himself up as best he could I informed dad I desperately needed the loo. On reaching the single loo below deck, well let's just say the sights that greeted us along with the putrid smell had me and dad hightailing it out of there. Dad took me back on deck in the hope the sea air would refresh me. As sick as I felt my mind kept returning to my pressing problem. As Dad was attempting to smoke his fag in what felt like a force 10 gale I prayed without too much conviction that I would hold on to my dignity until we landed in Dun Laoghaire. Sadly, without going into detail for the rest of the journey I hadn't a friend in the world. Even mum and dad kept telling me to go up on deck and air my pants.

Though vague as my childhood memories are about the Ireland trip, a few remain quite vivid; being hungry nearly the whole time we were there, collecting water from a stream's basin, the ever- present smell of cooked bacon - so tantalising for us hungry young kids, knowing it wouldn't end up in our bellies. Mum crying on the beach at Arklow, probably because of the realization she'd brought her kids across the Irish Sea in order for them to meet their ailing grandparents but maybe because our grandparents were struggling to cope with an influx of 10 more mouths to feed. Whatever, it wasn't the best of times but far from the worst, hunger apart, we really enjoyed it. Hunger is probably a little strong, we were fed, not the amount we were used to, but enough to keep body and soul together.

One day me and my sister Kathleen were pottering round the overgrown part of the large garden when Kathleen let out a scream and clung to me for dear life. What? What? A rat! A rat! It ran across my feet. Excited at the thought of a rat hunt I started searching through the undergrowth. After a while and tiring from my searching, I spied something dark, half hidden in the grass. On pushing the grass aside with my foot, I revealed not a skulking rat but a rusty old 'Jin trap'. For those not in the know a 'Jin trap' is a particularly brutal contraption for trapping animals, it comprises of interlocking metal jaws that, when forced open, revealed a small square metal plate. If you were to prod this metal plate with a stick it would snap together with real force and secure the stick in its vicious grip. Sadly me and Kathleen decided we'd try to catch Mr. Rat. Our plan was simple. After our meal we'd retain a piece of bread (a small piece!) and set the trap with our piece of lovely bread as bait. How could Mr. Rat resist?

That's exactly what we did and after waiting an hour or so we returned to where the trap was laid. To our surprise, while still a distance from the trap we heard the clash of metal on metal. Excitedly we raced to the scene but instead of finding a rat in our trap, to our horror, there was a robin stuck fast in the trap. Kathleen began screaming and shouting for me to free the little bird. Using all my strength I forced the jaws of the trap apart. To our delight the robin flew up and away towards the trees. It was only when we looked down at the trap that we realised the poor robin wouldn't enjoy a smooth landing. Sadly the bottom half of its legs were left in the trap. It was an awful feeling for the both of us. Kathleen was angry and sobbing through gritted teeth. We would suffer bad luck for the rest of our days. We'd killed the sacred bird that tried to help Christ on the Cross, or so the story goes. After spending that day and most of the next sulking, we made a pact that from then on we would always do all we could for the little birds, especially the robins.

This must have been such an emotional trip for dad. His mum and dad were both there to greet us. There frail appearance quietly upsetting Dad and Mum. Apart from the logistical nightmare of an invasion of 10 extra family members us kids were shocked at the Spartan way our grandparents lived. No electricity, no gas, no running water and from what I remember very little food. From the outside, their cottage, with a wood at the back, looked picture perfect. The large open fire to the right of the single downstairs room was utilised to its full potential. All the cooking, drying and heating were achieved from its dancing flames. The water would be collected from the basin of a nearby stream with strict instructions not to disturb the sediment at the bottom which would cloud the water. The water would then be boiled as it contained tiny red worm-like creatures that wriggled endlessly to the surface and back down to the bottom.

The little village of Avoca was breathtakingly beautiful but the following two weeks would be very testing for us visiting Kavanaghs. No luxuries whatsoever but to be fair for us younger ones at least, our time would be taken up with leprechaun hunts, gooseberry collecting and tree climbing. From Nana and Granddad's cottage us kids to our delight found you could see the ocean. After much pestering from us kids mum agreed to take us to Arklow beach. Mum warned us it would mean a very long trek. She wasn't kidding. Every mile or so we passed huge houses in acres of land. Obviously not everybody was poor in the Ireland of the 60s.

Mum was travelling light, just her handbag, so us kids weren't expecting a picnic. No bother! As we finally reached Arklow beach and after laying down the small blanket I had carried on the journey us kids set off running and shouting. My sister Margaret and young Michael were set on a shell hunt. Me and my sister Kathleen set out to find rock pools where we'd been told the crabs and other creatures hide out. We were having great sport. After a while I noticed Mum in the distance, her body language revealing she was upset. I told Kathleen I wouldn't be long and made my way back to Mum's side. She was crying. Why was Mum crying?: I'd never seen Mum crying. "Why are you crying Mum?" I asked her. She just pulled me to her and said she was OK but was still crying. I can't tell you how that, what seems like an insignificant incident, affected me. I never found out what the cause was but here I am a 57-year-old bloke and the thought of that scene can still upset me.

Mum and Dad would spend the rest of their lives in the roles that we knew them for, both grafting to make sure us kids never went without life's staples, had enough to eat and punishment when we deserved it. And a whole lot of love. They would always be there. What a comfort. How Mum turned out to be the best Mum in the world I'll never know. Born in Salford, to an alcoholic mother, her Dad apparently could sell sand to the Arabs. Sadly he was killed in a bicycle accident when Mum was young. Mum was in and out of foster homes and knocked from pillar to post. Her saving grace was her brother, my uncle John. He was one of those fellas who it just felt good to be around. Softly spoken, wise, and always had time for a chat. Mum's saviour.

Mum and Dad

Life with Mum and Dad was good for us siblings. The story of how Mum and Dad got together was by this time family folklore, it went like this: During the war Dad was working on London Bridge, Mum happened to pass by. And Mum, being a bit of a looker in her day, attracted Dads whistle and crucially for the future Kavanagh kids, Mum looked back and smiled. Dad was a handsome fella. That was all he needed, he laid his pick down, made a beeline for Mum and pleaded with her to meet him that night for a drink. And, as they say, the rest is history. Fate had played her hand. And it was to be a fruitful union, basically between two completely opposite characters. Mum was a very strong and social creature and well into my '20s I believed she had super powers. Whatever life threw at us Mum would somehow get it sorted. Obviously there were some things even Mum couldn't mend. Marriage breakdowns, which sadly weren't uncommon in the Kavanagh family.

Mum loved a good laugh. The thing was she had such a contagious laugh, everyone around her ended up in tears of laughter. I remember once being up town, walking along the rock with my mate, Brian Heys, when my ears picked up on the unmistakable sound of Mum in mid flow of a laughing fit. Looking across the street Mum and my sister Margaret were stood at a bus stop, watching a guy who probably had forgot his medication, towing a dog lead behind him, on the end of which was a large butcher's bone. The guy had stopped at the lamp post facing Mum and Margaret and was pulling a face as he waited for the bone to do its business. Why this scene tickled Mum and Margaret so much I'll never know. Then, good God, no, it couldn't be, but it was. Little puddles started to form between Mum and Margaret's feet. My mate pulling on my sleeve saying isn't that your Mum and Mags over there? To change the subject I pretended I'd lost my wallet and told him we'd have to retrace our steps. We parted from this embarrassing scene with me silent in the knowledge Bri was thinking "and since when have you carried a wallet?" Thankfully he decided to let it pass (families - don't they make you proud!).

Music and the Kavanaghs

Music seems to have always played a big part in our family life. Patrick was our self-appointed DJ; one of my earliest memories was one very hot sunny day me and my sister Margaret had borrowed Patrick's Dansette record player that allowed you to play 10 singles at a time, although it wasn't advised to adhere to this as the last single to fall onto the turntable invariably skidded.

Anyway, unbeknownst to Patrick we had a large selection of his singles that we were skimming through to find some of our favourites. Margaret loved Duane Eddy and anything by the Stones. She said they were much better than the Beatles as they had that elusive ingredient – menace. I found my favourite single at that time, a song called 'Just Like Eddy' by an artist called 'Heinz'. The song was written, as it turned out, about Duane Eddy. So Margaret loved it too. We were happily enjoying ourselves with the music when Mum called us in for our dinner. As we were finishing our dinner there came a knock at the door. Mum answered it. On her return she informed us there was a gang of kids out front asking if we wanted to join them in a game of 'kick the can'. Could you imagine trying to entice a group of today's kids to play "Kick the Can."

> "Right lads and girls, firstly we place a can on the floor. Next, we pick a guard. As the guard turns his back for a count of thirty, the rest of us scatter and find a place to hide. After finishing the count, the guard must seek the hidden. On locating them, a "tig" will ensure their capture and they must return to the can. The aim of the game is for the guard to capture everyone. But if, while the guard is away from the can, attempting to capture more playmates, any free player can appear from anywhere and "Kick the Can", he sets everybody free leaving the guard to start again. How good is that Kids? Kids!? – Kids!?"

I think me and Margaret left scorch marks on the kitchen lino as we sprinted out the door. There were about 18 of us, a complement of Holts, a brace of Mottershead and half a dozen Mahons. Lovely! The game went on for about three hours after which me and Margaret trudged wearily back home. After a refreshing drink of cold pop we made our way to the back garden to resume our record playing.

We were in for a shock. The 50 or so records we'd left scattered on the grass in our garden had taken on strange shapes. Some had acquired curled up wings, others had a curl at one end and a droop at the other. And guess what, it just had to be all our favourites bar one that were ruined. 'Running Bear' by Pat Boone had been completely hidden from the sun by the lid of the Dansette. Me and Mags just stared at one another. "God we're in a fix." Margaret's suggestion of putting them back in Pat's drawer and hoping for the best was a non-starter. My suggestion of saving our pocket money for as long as it takes to replace all Pat's records was greeted initially with some enthusiasm till Margaret reminded me we don't get pocket money.

In the end we collected all the disfigured singles up from the garden, put them back in their sleeves, well those that fitted, unplugged the record player, took them up to Pat's room and placed them neatly on his sideboard. We finally decided we would wait for Pat to come home from work and throw ourselves at his mercy and just hope he'd had a brilliant day at work. We explained to Mum what we'd done and how sorry we were and of our plan of repentance. She informed us it was a terrible thing to do to plunder your brother's privacy and add insult by damaging his records. Mum had no pity for us. Nervously we waited for Pat's arrival home. Normally a good humoured soul, we hoped today would be no different.

Around 8pm we could hear voices making their way by the side of the house to our back door. "Easy there Pat, don't try and put all your weight on it. "We recognised the voice of big Jim Booth, our Pat's mucker. Mum was there in a flash. "Oh, my God, what's he done Jim?" "Broke his ankle Mrs. Kavanagh. Some joker had placed a house brick inside a burst Frido ball on Huntley Mount Road on the footpath. Pat beat me to it and wellied it with all he had." That was enough for me and Mags. We were out the front door like we'd seen a banshee. We didn't return till it was going dark. Mrs. Fishwick up the street had let us sit with their Rita and Tommy and watch telly. Me and Mags always thought of the Fishwicks as posh, they even had a bowl of fruit when no one was ill. On our sheepish return, as our Pat's prone body took centre stage with his plaster cast-clad left foot raised up on a chair, there was no way to avoid it. "Well, well. It's my lovely sister and brother who's kindly decimated my lovely record collection." Because of my nerves or whatever I was about to laugh and then thought better of it. He continued: "as there's no way you can pay me back in money as you're both paupers, you'll both do my bidding while I'm laid up with my broken ankle." Mum agreed it was a fair trade off. Well he was good to his word; Pat had us chasing our tails for what seemed like years but actually was only five long weeks. A lesson learned.

Being a young fit lad, I found myself attracted to some of the girls on the estate. Strangely, on finding myself alone with any of them, I mostly felt awkward. With lads I knew how to act but with girls, well. I really liked my best mate's sister Yvonne, who happened to live next door. Of course she wasn't aware of this; when I'd spot her in her yard I'd make out I wasn't aware she was there and begin singing "Roses are red my love, violets are blue". It's a lovely song, I can't remember who sang it but anyway in my mixed up way of thinking I assumed Yvonne would catch on. Silly me.

Nevertheless on a lovely summer's day (we had a lot of them then) I'd erected a makeshift tent, basically two pieces of wood and a blanket thrown over it and another smaller blanket as a groundsheet. Mum placed her deckchair at the side of my tent, she then went back to the kitchen and brought out a large bowl and a smaller one. I knew from experience what she would be doing. In the large bowl would be a mixture of egg yolks and two other ingredients I can't remember, in the smaller bowl were some sliced cucumber. After applying the yolk mixture covering her face and neck Mum would then apply a piece of cucumber to each eye. She would then sit in the sun for an hour or two in which time the mixture set hard. And woe betide anyone who tried to force her into any facial expression, causing the cracks Mum was convinced would ruin the whole procedure.

Well, as I watched Mum apply the finishing touches a plan hatched in my childish but imaginative mind. I went in search of Yvonne and found her out front on her own, catching bees with a piece of cardboard and a jam jar. A pastime I enjoyed myself, why, I'm not sure. Still uncertain about Yvonne's feelings towards me, the words I'd rehearsed in my head rolled out in a mumble, anyway she must have caught my drift as she came along anyway. I'd attempted to inform Yvonne of Mum's peculiar beauty procedure and told her she must come and see her baking in the sun doing her impression of a hundred-year-old granny with the worst case of jaundice ever seen. Knowing we'd both end up laughing at Mum, but with the knowledge that Mum would stay silent, hopefully I could coax Yvonne into my tent just to be next to her for a while.

To my delight it was Yvonne who suggested we go into the tent, whispering in my ear "let's go in". Because of the size of the tent there was lying room only which suited me fine. It felt lovely. Suddenly Yvonne starts crawling all over me, whispering "baby" and planting kisses on the back of my neck. I was in a fix. Don't get me wrong, it felt lovely but I'd never kissed a girl properly and I wasn't about to start learning how with my Mum a yard away probably listening to Yvonne going on with herself. I had no idea what I could do so I stayed face down and pretended I'd fallen asleep. Thankfully Yvonne lost interest after a while and left me lying there. While Mum was still impersonating a jaundiced granny I sneaked out of the tent and sought shelter in my room where I did fall asleep dreaming of my chances of tempting Yvonne back to the tent which were, at best, pretty slim. The following day she was playing in her back garden, so with raised spirits I began to sing "Roses are red my love, violets are blue..ue...ue" when Yvonne, in a tense voice shouted to me "is that the only song you know?" Oh well.

Dad and the Blarney!

Mum and dad rarely argued. One reason I suppose was Dad was the classic Irishman in all ways except the one so common to his fellow countrymen – 'the gift of the gab'. He put this down to never kissing the Blarney stone. To be held by the ankles upside down while he laid a smacker on a rock that had been smooched by all and sundry, well! It just didn't appeal to him. Dad was content to sit in his comfy chair, observe his family and the rest of the world stumble along and keep his counsel.

The only time dad was animated was at the weekend after a few beers. One of the most comical sights I have witnessed, was on the occasions I had caught sight of dad making his way home after a night out in the Cotton Tree or Bluebell. In his outstretched hand, held like a precious thing, was dad's sweetener for mum – her fish and chips. The thing was, dad's legs were all over the show but the fish and chips never moved an inch. Unbelievable! Mum now and then had a dig at dad over the state he'd come home in. I had sympathy with dad, he grafted all week, never ever missed work, and never drank during the week. God bless him.

Scary Story

As I've already stated, life for a kid on the Dicky Bird estate was magic. The place was packed with kids who were happy in each other's company, playing the simple games of the day. There came a time when, for quite a while, my idyllic existence on the estate was darkened by a cloud that would take a good while to pass over and let the sun shine through again.

It all began when Dad gained some welcome extra work. It seemed the main reason Dad acquired the work was very simply because there weren't many takers. The nature of the work turning most men away. Dad's description went like this: he was to be part of a team relocating graves from the small cemetery at the side of Brunswick School on North Street, which now houses Woolfield Tesco, to Bury cemetery. Not all of the graves were relocated, some were left. Mum wasn't happy at all, asking Dad why in the world they were set on disturbing those resting souls. Dad limply mumbled something about the area being needed for some important development.

Well that was too much for Mum. Important development. "Well I hope to God it justifies desecrating dozens of graves. I pity the person who took this decision, their life will be blighted and what's more they'll deserve it." Dad, looking very sheepish, tried to justify himself. "Teresa! I'll earn more money in a few days than I would in a month navvying." Their eyes met and as they stared at one another something passed between them, unspoken but agreed on. Mum never fetched the subject up again. A few days after Dad finished his gruesome stint, although this information was to be kept strictly from the sensitive ears of us kids. Sadly, as often happens in these situations, someone blabbed. I was informed around a hundred coffins were fetched to ground level in varying states of deterioration. And I tell you now the next words struck fear into my young soul. Two of the coffin lids contained bloodstained fragments of fingernails embedded in the wood. Oh my God!

My very lively imagination was soon busy thinking horrible scenarios mostly ending with myself entombed alive in total darkness with little room and even less air. Vivid thoughts of my last moments have stayed with me till this day. I find it almost impossible to understand folk who go pot holing, squeezing through tiny gaps in the cave going deeper and deeper into the bowels of the earth. It amazes me anyone could enjoy this. It would be one of my worst nightmares.

In my last year of junior school Mum, don't ask me why, bought me and Kathleen matching anoraks embroidered with a flowery edging. I was about to explain to Mum I couldn't wear what was obviously a girl's coat when Mum went on one about how short of money we were at that time and maybe she was a bit hasty buying me and Kathleen our new coats. Kathleen whispered to me "forget it for now."

On our way to St. Joseph's I got into a fight with a couple of kids who were making fun of me in my new coat. You can imagine how it went. "Hi Girlie! How about a kiss?" After a minor scuffle which saw me and one of the boys stood with fully inflated lungs, chest to chest, each of us hoping to break the others nerves, Kath, who had seen and heard enough, without further ado, had both lads by the scruff of the necks, screaming that poor folk can't afford to be choosy, only happy with their lot and then she went on to the old 'sticks and stones' mantra. The two boys never uttered a word 'till Kath had set them free and were far enough away to feel safe.

All through her life outrage at injustice would always be a big part of her character. Epitomised one Sunday night at Bury FC social club. A dispute between two lads saw one of them reach for a pint glass before he could administer a sickening blow, he found our Kath hanging on the offending arm. To say the fella got a dressing down was putting it mildly. The word 'coward' was screamed into his face a couple of times. I can't tell you how proud I was of our Kath that night.

Emmie's Showrooms

The fashion of the day never really reached Dicky Bird estate. Certain articles trickled through, sky blue jeans were a real coup, black and white bumpers with the rubber side ankle protectors, well they were the bees knees. But mostly we were happy with whatever Mum fetched home from 'Emmie's Showrooms'. Emmie was a great friend of Mums. She lived on Lord Street that ran between Rochdale Road and Spring Street. Emmie's husband Harold was the local rag and bone man and one of the nicest, honest hard working blokes I've ever had the good fortune to meet.

One tale to sum him up began one day after returning back home after a long day collecting. While checking the pockets of one of the coats he was astonished to find £100 in £10 notes. Harold was the head of a family like many others, barely making ends meet. Harold was straight down to Bury police station, told the officer in charge what happened and left the money with him. Now a lot of folk would say, well that's what he should have done, isn't it. And of course it is. But there's many in Harold's position who would have succumbed to temptation. Anyway Harold and Emmie kept the younger members of the Kavanagh clan well turned out.

Church on Sundays

Sunday mornings were a chaotic time in the young Kavanagh household. To get the whole brood well turned out for Sunday Mass at 9am required almost military precision. But somehow Mum and Dad always managed it. Well Mum did anyway, Dad taking a passive role. Mary, the eldest of the siblings, was a great help to us younger kids. To be honest, church on a Sunday was a bit of a treat. We'd enjoy the trip to the little St. Bede's church on Rochdale old road where us younger kids could look for birds' nests in the hedgerows along the way. Plus we'd each pick a colour beforehand. Any car sporting any of our colours was added to your personal list.

The service itself was to be endured. For kids like us who were burning with energy it wasn't easy to spend over an hour expending no energy whatsoever, occasionally repeating a pray or an Amen. Then the collection came around where Mum would put an undisclosed sum onto the collection plate. Us kids always felt awkward at this time simply because we had nothing to donate. We explained to Mum our predicament and bless her, from then on we were all issued with a threepenny bit to cure our embarrassment.

Truth be told there wasn't a lot to interest a young kid during the service. Catholicism at that time was a very staid, uniformly glum religion based on fear as

Goldfinch Drive - us kids played games the full length of the street. The place was ALIVE. Meal times seemed an invasion of our fun.

much as joy. I can never remember leaving church feeling spiritually uplifted. Confession proved another trial. I was a kid living on Dicky Bird estate, compared to today in comparative innocence but each week us kids would attend confession where we'd kneel in the small cubicle with our priest sat likewise, with a partition containing a small grill between us, struggling to think of suitable transgressions to which the priest could pardon us. I was no saint but I admit most of my confession contained sins I wasn't even guilty of. I think the only time I enjoyed being a Catholic was during the Whit walks where we would be bought new clothes and walk through the streets of our fair town with a definite feeling of pride. Marching as an army along with my school friends, continuous clapping our constant companion. Yes we enjoyed that.

1965

1965 was to be a momentous year in so many ways. In our last exam at St Joseph's junior school, me and my mate Paddy Holmes had come joint top. Don't ask! Goodbyes to be said, and more changes coming. New school, also a new house. After sitting through our Eleven Plus, me and Paddy and our families were quietly confident we would do well when selections were made for our new school, "St Gabriels."

First things first, we were to move house. Sad as us young Kavanaghs were to leave Dicky Bird, we also saw this move as a new adventure. Our new home was a big Victorian gable end terrace. It was regally set in the middle of Oxford Street which stands just off Heywood Street, near the town centre. Apparently we were purchasing the house from a family called the Quinns (Irish folk). Whenever the Quinns came to visit mum and dad, strangely mum acquired a slight Irish brogue (if it helps). The princely sum of £1,000 was agreed on. As the Quinns had bought a large house round the corner on Wilson Street, lasting friendships were formed. It was an exciting time for us younger kids.

The new house was brilliant, upstairs a bathroom and four bedrooms of decent size. My own bed beckoned. Downstairs a roomy front room, an even bigger living room and kitchen, decent back yard along with a shed with 1/4 inch glass windows, and, best of all, a large cellar. At the time of moving it was full of empty wine bottles and assorted junk. After going over the house with a fine tooth comb us younger kids still had the area itself to explore. So, in the late afternoon of the first day in our new home, me, Kath, Margaret and eight-year-old Michael set off on our adventure. We'd only been walking a short while when we came across Whitehead Park, a well stocked park and two play areas with well kept bowling greens. Crazy golf, tennis courts and a huge green topped off with a huge meteorite. Well, we were told it was a meteorite, nestled to one side of the tennis courts.

After leaving the park we took the lane that would take us by St. Thomas's School. Past Sales's Farm and after following the path by a slow-flowing stream that led us to a large, single railway arch. We cautiously stepped through the entrance, immediately saw the tunnel, went on for at least 30 yards along with the stream babbling at our side. Kath and Margaret both advised that we should turn back now. There was no way I was turning back. A minute or so of coaxing the three of them, the four of us walked slowly to the light. The sight that greeted us at the end of the tunnel left us in delighted silence. Turner himself couldn't have painted a more inviting scene. To our left, behind a fence made from railway sleepers, rose a hill to a height of around 40 feet, while on our right, behind our companion, the stream, the other hill's twin. About 60 yards beyond,

My niece Melanie in front of our house in Oxford Street.

across our line of vision, ran the majestic river Roach and, beyond that, unbroken farmland. We felt blessed. Over the coming years we would all enjoy many hours along with our yet-to-be-found new friends in our new playground.

The day came around sooner than I'd have liked for me to enter the portals of the school that had given the older Kavanaghs a good education and grounding to enter the big wide world. The eldest, our Mary, was among the first set of pupils recruited for its opening in 1954 Margaret, my older sister, was still in attendance. The school was run on efficient disciplined lines, with Scottish stalwart Mr. Banks at the helm and Miss Lord, his deputy, in close proximity, along with a selection of other teachers. We tend to remember the ones who had a definite effect on us. Mine personally were, in order of effect, Mr. Tonge, Mr. Richmond, Wee Willy Harwood and Mr. Riley. All as different as could be.

A frightening time for any kid starting 'big' school. So much going through our heads. 'Will I fit in, will I be up to the work', and, the biggest question; 'will I make the football team?' Our Pat had already briefed me about 'Gab's' football, second only to the Lord himself. "And believe me lad you won't find it easy." Ominous words indeed. Well at least I had my old mate Paddy Holmes along for company. Turns out me and Paddy didn't do as well in our eleven-plus as we would have liked. We were both headed, not for 1A, our intended target, but to 1C, obviously a blow to our families.

But, among the football-loving lads of St. Gabriel's, academia came a poor second behind the beautiful game. As we were a little while off the trials for team selection, Paddy informed me he had a plan. Although quietly confident, as we had the standard we needed to meet, to be sure of making the team, in his words we'd have to be in "tip top shape." He then asked me who was the best defender I knew. "You" I replied. "And you're the best forward I know," he replied. The fact we were best friends, and, from a moment of madness with a penknife the previous year 'blood brothers' had no bearing on our opinions.

So, Paddy's plan, although simple, was to prove one of the most physically testing exercises I've entered into. It went like this. Twice, a week after school, along with our boots, we'd set off for the blessed turf of Hoyles playing fields. After placing coats about eight feet apart to form our nets I'd take the ball about 50 yards from the goal. Paddy would stand about 15 yards between me and the goal, facing me. I could trot, run or sprint with the ball. Paddy informed me, best pal or not, because of his pride, he'd do his damnedest to stop me. I must admit at that time I'd rather have faced anyone than Paddy Holmes. He had it all. Tall, athletic and slightly faster than me, which is probably the only thing I ever begrudged him. In the past I'd tried everything I could to beat him in a sprint just once, sadly for me, it was never to be. Nearest I came was catching his heel with my toe as he crossed the finish line.   One thing I knew, I couldn't let my respect for Paddy divert me from the job in hand, to combat his admirable qualities I had to use my own not-to-be sniffed-at gifts. Paddy's rule was that I had to be within 10 feet of the goal to score. The idea was to imagine I'd just received the ball, just inside the opponent's half, and all that stood between me and glory was Paddy. Well I was going to give him a run for his money! To begin with I decided to approach Paddy at speed and attempt to get him off balance. As I arrived within a couple of feet, square to him, I dropped by left shoulder and with my right foot dragged the ball in the same direction. I sensed Paddy's weight shift to his right foot, my timing had to be perfect. At the exact moment his weight shifted to his right, in a swift movement with the outside of my right foot, I took the place at pace to his left side. Unable to recover quickly enough, I was away to slot the ball into the empty net.

Now, as you can imagine, things didn't go so sweetly for the full two hours. Not only did Paddy on many occasions guess rightly which way I was going, even when he guessed wrong he was quick enough for a second bite. A formidable opponent indeed. At the end these twice-weekly exercises it was, in all honesty, a good fifteen minutes before either of us had the strength to grunt at one another as we wearily made our way home.

Me and Paddy were still coming to terms with our new big school which lay on the left bank of the Irwell near the start of the Bury Radcliffe canal. Our uniforms were dark blue along with white shirts, the girls with their smart pleated skirts. The girls had separate playgrounds but we shared classes. We looked the part. We learned early on with the lads it was all about football, forget knowledge. Most of us knew at that time we were factory fodder. Our plan was simple; leave school on schoolboy forms with the Shakers, then straight into the England team. Easy! Before that there was the task in hand of getting into the school team. Paddy's plan had primed us well. We were both quietly confident. We were in for a shock. St. Gabriel's was overflowing with football talent. Pele. Eusabio, Bobby Charlton, Alan Ball, Garincha, Gordon Banks, Bobby Moore, George Best were all present in one guise or another. These lads lived and breathed football. Even the kickabouts in the yard were full blooded and whoever got the man of the match in P.E., which was always football, was carried shoulder high all the way back to the locker room.

After the first year trials, me and Paddy were ecstatic to find we'd been selected for the team. Friendships were formed during this time that would last to the present day. There was one lad, named Sandro Nitti, a tiny little fella, but what a footballer! Four foot tall, cute as a button and with a lovely Italian twang. Sandro would reveal to me my first ever witnessing of a perfectly executed overhead kick. What a sight! I was astounded. He seemed to be so high off the ground and met the ball perfectly to send it flying into the top corner. Our opponents that day were Seadfield. Immediately after Sandro's goal it was a couple of their lads congratulating him before we got to him. Sadly, because of the pressure for places in the team, Sandro most probably because of his small stature ended up being a fringe player. But what a fringe player! The star of the team was a lad called Nello Oliviero, I know another Italian, also our most graceful player; the comparisons with the more famous man Pele, to me, weren't that far fetched.

Bobby Charlton came in the form of Chris Long, a tall lean lad topped with a mop of red hair. Chris could hit a ball harder than anyone I knew. The fact that Chris wasn't a forward never prevented him from notching a decent quota each season. Alan Ball was present in the guise of Ged McLoughlin. A terrific fella, attributed with three lungs who tackled like a wolverine. Jack Charlton was mirrored by my mucker Paddy Holmes, a tall lean, uncompromising fullback, as already recorded in these pages. Paddy gave no quarter. Our left winger, Tony Holt, in my opinion, was one of the most underrated players in Bury. It's hard to liken Tony to any of the pro players of the day. He was a one off. Fast as you like, he could kick with either foot. I've seen many a fullback just glad to reach the safety of the changing rooms after facing him. I myself slipped in on the right wing, and, looking around me at my teammates, didn't envy our opposition. Mick Tonge was the teacher responsible for team training and team selection, sometimes aided by Mr. Richmond. No mean players themselves. When Friday came along, until I'd checked my name was in the first eleven of the team sheet I couldn't settle.

Around this time a new boot the Timpson Shooting Star, a boot that wouldn't look out of place on the feet of one of today's stars, low cut with moulded studs, blue tags on the heel and three blue stylish stripes on the side and comfy as a pair of old slippers were introduced. A couple of years later the revolutionary George Best boots came on sale, they were purple and black, laced up at the side. I preferred the 'Shooting Star'.

Expectations were high on the football front at St. Gabriel's, if any of the teams representing each year lost a game it would be a talking point for the rest of the following week. Each team was expected to win their respective leagues and the cup. Things usually ran to form; a rare exception was during our third year season. On a snowy November Saturday morning, we played Eastward in the cup and were defeated 0–1. Me and our midfield maestro, Ged McLoughlin, were so devastated by our defeat we retreated, still in our kits, to the seclusion of the gym to bawl our eyes out. As we were just getting ourselves together Mr. Tonge found the two of us in our sad state. His advice to us was short but not sweet. When you leave school and play with the big boys, this will happen often, he told us. "Get used to it."

An Unholy Match

In later years when we settled in Oxford Street we joined the parish of St. Marie's. I thought the church was lovely and unusual. Its circular bell tower I'd never seen the like of. As time went by I ended up helping out Father Fitzgerald by passing prayer books and doing any other menial tasks he asked of me. Father Fitzgerald was always civil and polite but as with most Catholic Priests I had the acquaintance of, was mostly unapproachable. Priests in our young minds were placed firmly on a moral pedestal almost, an alien breed and 'never the twain'.

These thoughts were to be shattered in my last year at St. Gabriel's. A football match was arranged between local priests and a team made up of local teachers, which in itself I found astounding - the thought of our pious collection of ministers going toe to toe with our teachers, some of whom weren't half bad footballers. And what's more it was to be played on our very own field of dreams, the St. Gabriel's playing fields. There was no way I was going to miss this.

The match planned for the following Friday afternoon at 4pm kick-off, I arrived at the pitch side with my best pal Paddy Holmes, we took our places to join a decent crowd busy chatting about the forthcoming event. Me and Paddy noticed, among the ranks of the holy fathers, were a couple of our school hero's, Ivan Crossly and my personal hero, Manuel Malesky, a big bustling centre forward with more under his bonnet than most mere mortals. Apparently this was a necessary move as enough physically equipped priests could not be found.

The referee blew the whistle to start proceedings on this most unusual football match. The first thing that struck us after about 15 minutes was the full blooded tackles that the clergymen's side were receiving, it seemed no quarter was being given to God's messengers. Mr. Riley, our Irish-English teacher (if that makes sense) seemed to me to be on a mission to put as many priests in our local hospital Bury General as he possibly could. This was a surprisingly bad tempered match with both teams determined to be the victors. Why it was this way I've no idea, but it certainly put an edge on a game I was expecting to be just a fun spectacle.

The referee, who I didn't know, was having his work cut out just keeping order, which probably came as a shock to him as well. Proceedings came to a head just before half time, Fr. Fitzgerald and our PE teacher Mr. Tonge both went up for a high ball, as Fr. Fitzgerald's feet regained the turf Mr. Tonge's feet came down on top of the priests. The air went blue with language to make a sailor blush. Me and Paddy just stared at one another, dumbfounded. Paddy commented "maybe Fr. Fitzgerald will be in the queue with us for confession next week." After which we both had a good laugh.

With Mr. Tonge looking somewhat chastened the second half began still with no score. This was all to change when 20 minutes into the second half a left wing cross from our maths teacher Mr. Richmond was headed gleefully home by the geography teacher, Mr McConville. The goal was immediately followed by a clap of thunder that I don't mind admitting scared me witless. Now you can imagine the comments from the assembled crowd. Laughter filled the air as one wise guy shouted at the priests' team as they took their places for the restart. "Well Fathers that's the boss letting you know what he thinks." The laughter subsided with the coming of the expected downpour. A few of the fainter hearted ran for cover to the nearby school building but there was no way me and Paddy were missing any of this match.

Gradually the priests were asserting themselves as the tackling in the wet conditions sometimes forced you to close your eyes and open them, praying all was well. Each clap of thunder seemed to spur on the clergymen. Me and Paddy found ourselves rooting for the priests' team as they were on the receiving end of some dubious tackling which to this day baffles me and Paddy, whether something had gone on beforehand I couldn't say. But without a shadow of doubt there was some sort of grudge involved in this match. After another caution for one of the teachers that followed a tackle that left a clergyman prostrate with his face in the mud the game looked like it would end with a win for the teachers.

Then, with a couple of minutes to go the star of the clergymen, a very young Fr. Williams, the only priest I ever knew to wear a United scarf under his cassock reading a gospel according to Brian Robson, collected the ball on the right wing and skipped by two defenders then floated a lovely cross that passed over the heads of the whole defence which found Manuel Maleski on the edge of the box. Manuel hit the ball on the volley. Me and Paddy already had our arms in the air. What we witnessed next was a comical string of events. The volley travelling around waist high saw Fr. Fitzgerald airborne, flying through the air attempting a flying header, the momentum carried him through the mud, settling alongside the goal line, the ball after hitting the far post settled by the side of his head. It was almost like time stood still as me and Paddy tried to will the ball over the line with the teachers for a split second hesitating. That split second saw Fr. Fitzgerald like a tadpole caught by the tail flick his head to send the ball over the line and me and Paddy into raptures.

And, believe it or not, at that moment the sun decided to make an appearance, coating all the assembled in a golden glow. A very fitting end to a very good if strange afternoon.

Trip t' Mill

Life at home was going well. Mary, the elder, was enjoying married bliss, brother Pat had a job with the local building firm Greenwoods, Sheila and Margaret both had jobs with Asworths Slipper Works. John had gained employment at a cotton mill just round the corner on James Street. One day while off school with some minor ailment I accompanied John to his place of work. As my presence wasn't questioned, I assumed security was a little loose.

My lasting memory is of the noise and Victorian machinery like a giant concertina opening and shutting. Occasionally a thread would break. I was informed the act of reconnecting the thread was called 'piecing up'. Before we left for dinner, with John's help, I was a decent 'piecer up'. Years later this skill would come in very handy when I joined the workforce of Scapa Yarns. Hard work by any standards. As things were, Mum had a little more money. One thing was for sure, it wouldn't go on herself.

Star Addition

The school team according to Mr. Tonge was doing OK. One problem we had was, for all our flair and undoubted talent, we weren't scoring that many goals. Then, as if heaven sent, a lad named Barry Allen whose family moved from his native Coventry arrived. His parents took over the Star pub in Freetown, one of Bury's small industrial areas. (Home to Bury's first ever gasworks.)   Barry joined us in class 3B and with his lively character and infectious laugh was almost straight away accepted as one of the lads. It was at his first P.E. lesson (football) that our new apprentice was to cause a near sensation. Barry was the first lad I'd come across who, when attired in football boots and kit had absolutely nothing on his mind, from his near immediate selection to the school team (a great feat in itself), but scoring goals. With Barry it was goals all the way. Now this wasn't to say he was one of those players who contracted hearing problems on receiving the ball, that would be an injustice. The lad had a lot more to offer. He was also a great team player but - if Barry could see the white of the 'keeper's eyes, forget it.

The Mad Lad Johnny Bugeja

Barry was a character who joined a school already teeming with characters. Thinking back, the craziest of these characters was classmate Johnny Bugeja. When I think of Johnny, an involuntary smile comes to me. A good looking lad, my sisters were always very attentive to Johnny when he came to our house.

There were two main incidents involving Johnny I could never forget. The first began on a cold January day. The day before Johnny had suggested going fishing on Elton Reservoir. Just him, his girlfriend Stephanie and me. Early the following morning found us already set up. We'd chosen the small lodge joined to its larger partner by a small stream. We'd chosen this place as we were enclosed by bushes which kept the worst of the constant cold breeze off our backs. Well there we were, me and Johnny, about 12 feet apart eyes fixed on our floats, hoping for a bite, mainly that's what fishing's about but also so Stephanie wouldn't be bored.   About an hour and a half passed. Nothing. Suddenly Johnny jumped up off his basket, beckoned Stephanie to take his place and, after giving her a minute's condensed lesson on the art of fishing, he left us, saying he wouldn't be long. Picture the scene; me and Stephanie side by side in peaceful silence. Staring hopefully at our respective floats, when slowly from our left into our line of vision glides a small plank of wood. Not too unusual you'd think. But this small plank of wood's cargo - well, let's just say it was still steaming. Me and Steph both fell off our baskets holding our bellies. As we looked at each other, tears of laughter streaming down our faces just set us off again. On Johnny's return after another laughing session we decided to pack up and leave Elton Reservoir to its former tranquillity.

My City Dream Over

Back to school and after the scout from Manchester City had visited mum and dad, I found myself a member of Whitehill boys (City's nursery team). To reach Sandy Lane, their home ground, I needed to take three buses which if I am honest I hated. I was never a confident traveller, being content to live life within the boundaries of the town of Bury. On a couple of occasions our Pat came along which was great. Alas most of the time I would be alone.

The other lads gathered from far and wide seemed to me to be reluctant to make friends. Ah well as long as they passed to me, which to be fair they did. The one lad who was friendly was Bobby Corrigan, the younger brother of Joe, who was also a 'keeper. The fella looking after us was called John Broom. As the months passed I asked John about the future; he would tell me just to carry on working hard.

This situation went on for many months. Mum was pushing me to force John to make a decision. During this time the day came to leave school. Easter 1970. On the final day, after many handshakes, hugs from the girls and promises to keep in touch and not be strangers, I was left in quite an emotional state. I suppose it is always sad, the end of anything but it wasn't just school. I had to face the fact that my dream of playing pro football was fast fading and it looked ominously like I would have to go out into the big bad world and earn a living. This came to pass a few months after leaving school I decided either because I just didn't have what it takes or John's focus on getting the best out of his young prodigies was lacking. I will never be quite sure.

Clarence Athletic

While playing for the school team I had also been turning out for a local outfit Clarence Athletic. They were managed by a character called Stuart Johnson, a cracking enthusiastic fella. From his home on Manchester Road, literally from his home, we'd change then make the short trip to Blackford Bridge Park where we would do our training under Stuart's supervision. A couple of lads stood out for me, each for different reasons.

Pete Johnson because he was such good company and one Anthony Cohen. Anthony was a great little player. To me he was another Franny Lee, pacey and very direct, his tactic of running at defenders at pace was a joy to watch. He could also hit a ball with either foot. I can't remember ever playing in a match alongside Anthony without him scoring. That is some feat. At one time we had no changing rooms due to an arson attack. We ended up along with our opposition getting changed in a derelict house in Warth Road that led onto our pitch under the arch by McPhersons Mill, literally on the banks of the River Irwell. On a couple of occasions the Irwell broke its banks, completely submerging our pitch. The only things having any sport on those occasions was a handful of seagulls.

Time to earn a living

Within a couple of weeks came a time when Mum turned to me with these immortal words:

"Eamon I've got you a job, you start at Antlers on Monday."

"You sure you don't want me to help 'round the house instead, Mum?" The look was enough.

Now I knew a little about Antlers, because I'd been knocking about with the Alfred Street gang who at that time compromised Harry Chadwick, Mick Greenacre, Glen Fothergill and Sandra Derbyshire (yes, a girl.) Harry was already working at Antlers. He likened his job on the production line riveting suitcases to the old chain gangs without the luxuries! Asking why he worked there then his reply was that the girls outnumbered the guys 10 to one! Suddenly I was quite looking forward to Monday. So one Monday morning in July 1970 I set off on the short journey from my home in Oxford Street to my first ever place of work, Antlers Pilot Mill on nearby Alfred Street. It was without doubt an imposing building, a very large four-storey Victorian cotton mill originally, Mum having spent some time working there when cotton was still king.

Now housing a luggage firm that began life in the Midlands, Birmingham to be exact, it was, apart from a couple of breaks to seek my fortune elsewhere, to be my working home for the next 16 years. As I passed through the main gates and approached the security cabin, to say I was nervous would be an understatement. Would I be able to do the job, would my work colleagues accept me? I was so deep in thought I hardly heard the security man say "Can I help you?" "I've come for a job" I stammered. He directed me to a corner of the building where I'd find a lift. I was to take the lift to the third floor and ask for Alan Holden. I followed these instructions and, upon reaching the third floor, the door slid open and standing there was a giant of a man who introduced himself as the man I sought. Alan told me the guy on security had phoned through to tell him of my arrival. He then showed me where to hang my coat. After this I was paraded around what would be my work area, being introduced to my future workmates. At times like this you can't help feeling a wally.

Two of the lads I was introduced to were Jim Berry and Sid Colson. They were doing a job called 'pulling on'. This required them to pull what seemed a very tight-fitting canvas cover over a hardboard frame. After performing this far-from-easy task they would then take a small circular brush, dip it in a crude-looking hot glue pot, then spreading it on the inside of the frame before proceeding to push the overlapping material on to the glue. I couldn't help noticing their calloused hands. These lads worked hard. I was beginning to have doubts. My mind was eased when Big Al informed me that I would be the production line gofer. This suited me as I thought at least my days would be varied, I could also be a social butterfly and get to know everyone. Apart from one or two, the folk there were brilliant and overall I'd enjoy working for Antler luggage and, over the years, so would several of my family.

Huntly FC

At this time on Saturdays at least I was in football limbo. Our Pat's words of advice were "you must play in the best standard you can. Keep yourself in the shop window." Wise words indeed, you'd think. If I'd have had the luxury of foresight I'd have just played in local football with my mates. Alas, it wasn't to be. To be fair, things started okay. A team called Huntley were interested in signing me. At the time they'd applied for Manchester league status, which, at the time, for a Bury amateur side, was a big step. Huntly was run by a big lovable bear of a man, Phil Carruthers. A nicer man you'd never meet. At the time they'd just left their original pitch, Grundy playing fields near Blackford Bridge, and acquired new grounds at the 'Old Doctors' behind Totty Con club just off Royds street in Tottington. Now the pitch, although enclosed by white painted metal rails (a Manchester League requirement) couldn't be mistaken for Wembley. There was a great hump in the middle of the pitch, like they'd buried Goliath there and the ground hadn't quite settled. But there's always a silver lining – it was never waterlogged, the water would just run off the hump behind the nearside goal. There were half a dozen half-finished houses. Apparently the building firm had run out of money. To me personally these derelict houses did nothing for match day atmosphere.

Some of the Huntley players were already known to me, players like Brian Wilcox, better known as 'Snowy'. Sadly, Brian passed away some time ago while still in his prime. Brian's passing rocked the local amateur football fraternity and a lot more besides. They say the good die young and they don't come any better than 'Our Snowy'. Another player known to me was Barry McCool. Mr. Magoo. A real character. After his playing days Barry, who, let's say, put himself about a bit, to everyone's surprise became a referee, and a pretty good one. The unique fact about Huntly F.C. was in our second season. We acquired the services of a new manager. The new man's name was Roy Freeman. Roy seemed to me a nice enough fella, and a very determined one. He being a Manchester lad, shocked all us Bury brigade by fetching with him at his first training session, half a dozen Manchester footballers.

As you can imagine, this put a few noses out of joint and created some bad feeling on the way. But, as with most things, as we got to know each other, good friendships were formed. And the bottom line was the new lads strengthened the squad. I enjoyed my time at Huntley, Roy put together a team that played good football. The players that stood out for me were Alan Whitmore, a tall lanky centre forward who played with craft and was a top marksman. Kevin Bryant, a good old fashioned centre back who played with his heart on his sleeve, Alan Bell, a complete utility man with

Huntly FC, 1974. This was a defining time in amateur football in Bury. Along with the appointment of Roy Freeman as manager, there was an influx of Mancunian talent to our little town.

a good engine, Ian Mcool who played sweeper, a very intelligent player – a players' player, and Liam Morrissey who must have been a love child of Nobby Stiles, a great competitor.

As far as I'm aware, Huntley was the first team in Bury to bring in Manchester lads en masse. Around this time my younger brother Michael was flowering into a decent little footballer. That season Huntley began running a reserve team and Michael fought his way into it. An intelligent lad, he was the only Kavanagh to ever carry a briefcase, a fact we never let him forget. In the meantime, Roy Freeman's hard work and belief in us paid off. We won the final of the Gilchrest Cup on Manchester's county ground, a great achievement.

Night Ratting

At Antlers my working life had improved. I had my own job fitting locks, handles and feet to the suitcases, I'd also achieved a level of performance, along with 90% of my fellow workmates that would give us a small bonus, small being the operative word. Unless you got into management or worked every hour God sends, you weren't going to get rich at Antler! Thank God there were other bonuses. My work colleagues were lovely folk and with the work being so simple and mundane you could dream. My workplace by the windows on the third floor allowed a panoramic view of the countryside. At the back of the mill the seven arches that carried the old Bury to Heywood line beneath which the river Roach meandered its way passing Water Farm then flowing directly behind Antlers mill and on to Goshen playing fields. On those banks I would spend many hours in pursuit of the rat, either on my lonesome or in the company of friends. I considered myself among the last ratters in town. My Jack Russell dog Tina was marking holes consistently. My ferret Percy was doing a grand job and my rifle, a BSA Meteor .22, for the price, was the best rifle on sale at that time.

The rifle I always wanted, but could never afford, was the BSA Airsporter 22. The Rolls Royce of air guns. There was just something about ratting; walking along the banks of the Roach or Irwell, seeing all the other wildlife, resting on the banks for a breather and a bite to eat, just enjoying nature. (Admittedly killing some of it, my only defence is that it was vermin).

Something that I'd never done at this point was gone ratting at night. This was to change when I got to know Sid Colson who worked on 'pulling on'. Sid was a lovely fella. A Brummie who came up from Birmingham with the firm, he was a real lively character; he also shared my love of air guns and hunting. When he suggested going out at night I was interested right away, just the practicalities had me puzzled. On the night we chose I called round to Sid's Rhulas Drive home. He proceeded to show me what was needed. First, with a small wood chisel, he scraped the sulphur off the ends of a pile of matches. My puzzled look brought a smile to his face. He then proceeded to use a blunt pencil to force the sulphur into the cavity of the gun pellets. Still puzzled, he promised me all would be revealed. After taping torches to the underside of our gun barrels, coats on, Tina on lead, we were off for the banks of the Roach. We decided night-time was not the time to be using a ferret.

As we reached the banks of the Roach, and moved further away from any form of light, I can't speak for Sid, but I admit I found it scary. We had the light from the torches on the barrels of our guns, but to me they made everything look even more eerie. Sid sneakily dropping pellets into the water near me didn't help. After he agreed to quit we

Me with two of my ferrets, Percy on my left!

set about the job in hand. Suddenly Tina let out a short bark then the unmistakable plop of a rat entering the water, what normally happens here, the rat will keep to the banking, alighting further downstream or more often swimming underwater as long as it could to reach the opposite bank, because of the width of the Roach the rat would break surface a couple of yards short of the bank. This was the time for the marksman to choose. Sid raised his rifle to eye level and his beam of light fell onto the back and head of the part submerged rat about 20 yards away from us, Sid fired and a red dot of light travelling at a fantastic speed ended its journey with a thud and the instant death of the rat. I'd never seen anything like it; these tracers as Sid called them were fantastic. Tina swam the 20 or so yards to retrieve the rat's body. On reaching the bank where me and Sid were stood she proudly dropped the rat at our feet then proceeded to shake herself, soaking both of us.

That night we travelled as far as The Arches then made our way back, by this time our eyes had become accustomed to the dark which made the return journey a little easier. Night ratting, although different and enjoyable but because we'd be arriving home in the early hours was only practical at certain times. I came to really admire Sid, he was a bloke with a head full of interesting things who was more than willing to share them. He also played the guitar which I was so envious of. On the few occasions I turned up at his for some lessons we'd end up jabbering on about this and that, for obvious reasons our taste in music was discussed. Turns out they were very similar 'Country/Irish' and the living legend 'Johnny Cash'. My whole family loved Johnny. They had to – our Pat forced it on all of his siblings. So because of this, love or hate would be the result as it turned out we all loved him to this day and many concerts later. So me and Sid would share our stories into the night while Kay, his lovely wife, kept us fed and watered. "Another brew flower?" in her endearing Welsh brogue, while the guitars sat all night, gathering dust.

Country vs Soul

By the time we'd moved to Oxford Street my musical tastes were influenced largely by our Pat which was mostly American country. I was also influenced by friends who, like me, loved music and saw it as part of who they were.

Any member of the gang who'd found the money to buy a new single, well we'd all be round theirs playing it to death until we more or less knew the words or if we didn't, substituted a word that fit nicely. One day one of the gang, Christine Dell, turned up with a portable record player. It resembled a narrow toaster with a slot that accommodated singles only and only one at a time but it was a revelation. We'd all fetch our favourite singles and beg Christine to play them as we walked the streets around Pimhole. As each individual acquired listening rights they'd insist on silence as their single was played, frowning if anyone so much as breathed heavily. All except when my single was on! I grudgingly understood their reaction, after listening to soul and Motown classics my offering for the night would begin and almost instantly there'd be "What the f**k? Turn that shite off. Who the f**k is Hank Williams anyway?"

Looking back I understand them but at the time I took it very personally. Some of the arguments I still remember. Attempting to defend playing "Your cheating heart" by Hank Williams – "Eamon, why would we want to listen to a song about some guy who's missus keeps cheating on him, it's depressing." "Well 'Tears of a Clown has just been playing and you were all singing along with it!' "That's not depressing!" A bloke crying his eyes out, not depressing? "No, it's like listening to the blues, these black folks can sing about sad things but it ain't depressing." "Well country is white man's blues and I don't find it depressing."

Truth is, for a while I quit listening to country music in order to be one of the in crowd. Which, looking back, was daft. You should never be embarrassed about what music you like. Whatever pleases your ears.

I look at my collection now and to say the least it's diverse. I love '60s music, Meat Loaf, Swing, UB40, Eminem… Anything that pleases my ears. But even now the bulk of my collection is made up of country and Irish. Music to me has to affect you in some way, otherwise its just background noise. It should make you smile, make you cry, make you think, relax you, make you want to dance. Change your mood. I love powerful songs that sometimes make the hairs on the back of your neck stand up. A couple of songs come to mind. 'Green Fields of France' by Davy Arthur and the Fureys. Every time I hear it I get emotional for different reasons. Penny Lane has the same effect. And there's a '60s anti-war song by a fella called Barry McGuire named 'Eve of Destruction' – the sheer emotion in McGuire's voice is frightening. This tale of the futility of war is sung with the undisguised anger it deserves. Fabulous.

During the '70s there were two stalls on Bury outside market where you could buy records. The one in the centre of the market was run by a fella who used an old ambulance to transport his stock. It was OK but he just seemed to regurgitate the same stuff. The good thing was he would play music to the passing shoppers. It was there I first heard Charlie Pride's 'Chrystal Chandeliers', a very catchy song. I purchased the album and was well happy with my acquisition. The other shop was situated to one side of the market as one end was blocked with a wall, it was like entering a garage. The fella who had this stall tended to keep well up with current trends. Me, along with a couple of the lads, had recently begun a love affair with soul music which happily lasts till this day. My mate Bry Heys loved Otis Redding to the point of distraction. One night, while having a drink in his attic bedroom on Heywood Street, he insisted I listen to a track called 'These Arms of Mine'. I can honestly say it blew me away.

You could close your eyes and literally float away on a cloud of sweet soul emotion. During this period I acquired a whole lot of soul singles and albums most of which have disappeared over the years. Among the survivors is the first ever soul album I bought priced at 99p. It was a real bargain. 'This is Soul' is a cracker. Another is 'Jimmy Ruffins Greatest Hits'. They don't come better than Jimmy. The only problem for me, as far as music was concerned was, as I didn't own my own record player, I could only use the communal one in our living room in Oxford street. It was time I had my own. This would mean some serious saving, hampered by the low wages I received at Antlers. I decided it would be worth it to have my very own record player. I'd keep it in the bedroom I shared with my older brother. John wasn't passionate about music, so I figured he wouldn't interfere when I fancied a musical evening. It would be four long months before I'd find myself at the door of Norman Helms on Silver st. That two pounds religiously put away each week, now amounted to £32.00, safe in my back pocket.

With the help of a very attentive sales assistant I settled on what he informed me was for the price the pick of the bunch. Radio and tape recorder to compliment a turntable that although top of the range would only accept one record at a time, L.P. or single, the multiple record holder, now considered dated. On arriving home with my precious cargo courtesy of a mates work van. I can't tell you how excited I was setting it up in my room. Finally all was set. Now what record do I choose to grace my virginal turntable, after some deliberating I settled for "Silvia's Mother" by Dr. Hook, I just love that song. And man it sounded good. Many hours were spent in that room transferring many of my records onto tape, the benefit being it gifted you longer playing time. Many of those tapes survive in my collection today.

Footy at Rocky Rd.

Although playing Saturdays in a competitive league, I really looked forward to my midweek trips to Rochdale Road Park where there would be a gathering of anything from 20-30 lads itching for a kick about. A young kid showing talent way beyond his years had seasoned players talking excitedly about him. That kid was Paddy McSherry. Paddy would become a legend in the ensuing years as he would mature into one of the finest defenders Bury non league players would ever see. A commanding figure who demanded respect (and got it!) with a steely determination that was infectious to his team mates. With Paddy in your side you always had a chance. Another young kid turning heads was Mick Williams (Willy). Mick in future years would become an inspiration to his team mates.

These kickabouts at Rocky Road would carry on late into the evening. By the time someone reluctantly said those immortal worlds "next goal winner". Instinct and knowledge of the pitch took over from vision and with some of the lads your sense of smell was a real asset. A "luminous ball" in those days would have been priceless. After the games we'd all make our weary way home. Needless to say trouble getting off to sleep was unheard of. Rocky Road Park would continue to be a place of enjoyment. Me and my mate Brian Heys in the summer holidays would spend hours in the park, utilising all its facilities including tennis, bowls and crazy golf. After we'd had our fill of the games, we'd make the short journey to the Roach Pub facing the park, it was a time when a lot of people started going abroad for their holidays. Much to our delight this meant the pubs me and Brian frequented on Rochdale Road, The Roach, the Peel Hotel, The Crown and the Seven Stars were mostly nearly empty. No queuing for a pint, pool or the dart board. Brian was a great lad, great company and possessed a wicked sense of humour. Brian's family arrived in Bury from 'Back of the Moss' a rough part of Heywood. Brian could certainly handle himself and I secretly thought he quite enjoyed a rumble.

There was one time he had a "set to" with an ex school mate, Tony Fierro. The place they chose to settle their disagreement was, where else, Rochdale Road Park. When two hard lads meet head on something's got to give, but not on this occasion. The best reflection I could give you is, if you were lucky enough to see the film 'The Quiet Man' – the fight scene had definite comparisons. And, as in the film with John Wayne and Barry Fitzgerald, Brian and Tony, after a long hard battle were left with both their dignities intact. Brian's family had settled into one of the big houses on Heywood Street. Mum, Dad, (Brian Snr.), two sisters and three brothers, Brian acquired the attic bedroom. He made it his own with his music, mostly 'country' and his own wardrobe containing some tasty gear, Brian was irresistible to the girls, sometimes I'd pass a girl on her way down the stairs looking very content.

One time, on reaching Brian's door, I was greeted by a padlock hanging open. On asking him about said padlock he said it was to keep his younger brother Clifford from gaining access, as, on a couple of occasions, he'd caught Clifford raiding his stash of sweets. Within a week he would catch Clifford red-handed in his bedroom, Brian having to stride over a screwdriver and screws before entering his room. On thumping Clifford to the ground, Clifford had got up and proceeded to throw punches at Brian. Brian had finally got Clifford's face down with his arm up his back, promising no more trespassing. We knew then Clifford would grow into one tough cookie and in later years, after a run in with Brian in Bury's Atmosphere nightclub, would remind his older brother just how tough.

Breaking the Humdrum

On the working front, as I've said, work at Antlers was mind numbingly boring, working on a production line didn't require too much imagination, in fact the less the better. Because of the boredom, practical jokes were a great release for the comatose work force. I remember taking a tape recorder up to the bedroom I shared with my older brother John. John was out back either taking apart or putting back together one of the many motorbikes he had over the years, this one being a Triumph Bonneville. Anyway I knew I wouldn't be disturbed.

I placed a blank cassette into the holder then pushed the play button, after letting it run for a couple of minutes, I then proceeded to knock on my wardrobe door at the same time calling "let me out" "please let me out it's dark in here", keeping this up for around four minutes. At the earliest opportunity I secreted the tape recorder inside a suitcase on a conveyer belt awaiting inspection. The inspector on this day was a large German lady named Magda. Magda was a stickler for quality and there's something about her German accent that made her appear a little stern.

Well picture the scene. The case being pushed along, all the time getting nearer Magda's inspection bench. I was working a good 20 feet from the case that was now next to Magda. I noticed her head kept jerking to her right. She then stopped what she was doing, walked a couple of paces, cocked her head to one side like a confused puppy, and then let out a scream that brought everyone to a standstill. In her loud German accent Magda was screaming that there was someone in the suitcase. The people in the know were in stitches, the others seemed just as frightened as Magda. The commotion reached the ears of our production manager Alan Holden, order was regained after Alan bravely opened the suitcase to reveal the offending machine. It didn't take long to trace the prank to myself. Within minutes I found myself in Alan's office. I survived the 20 minute grilling; it wouldn't be the last.

Gilchrest Cup

The following Wednesday was to be a big one in my football calendar. Huntly had a quarter final Gilchrest Cup match against local rivals Prestwich Heys at our ground, the Old Doctors The game was a lively affair, one of those games that was a joy to play in, no quarter given, cracking goals and played at 100 miles an hour. A proper English game. Ten minutes to go it was 2–2 with both sides pressing, also trying to keep things tight. The majority of the players were mentally accepting a draw and, to be honest, it would have been a fair result. But as is so often the case someone hadn't read the script.

That someone was Alan Bell. Alan picked the ball up just outside his own penalty box, avoided two tackles which took him past the half way line. After nutmegging their captain everyone expected Alan to pass the ball if for no other reason than sheer exhaustion. Prestwich's defence rushed forward as a unit. As their centre half confronted Alan he pushed the ball straight through his open legs. As their 'keeper came rushing out Alan, without breaking steps, with the toe of his boot coolly lifted the ball over the 'keeper into the net. I knew I'd witnessed something special. How do you describe that feeling? I felt like bursting, I wasn't sure with what. What Alan felt like after a goal like that I can only guess at. Once he reappeared from under a mass of teammates bodies we just looked at each other with gormless grins on our faces. "Football – Magic aint it?"

After the game I was introduced to our newest arrival from the Manchester contingent, a lad called Tommy Allen. Tommy was no mean footballer but to me Tommy's talent lay in the finer points of the game. Tommy being an easy going affable Irishman who somehow demanded respect. And respect Tommy got from everyone lucky enough to know him. With Tommy in the team it just felt better. My strongest memory of Tommy will always be the fact he was the only living person to actually take me to one side to give me a few pointers which he considered would help my game, for which I will always be thankful. Tommy would eventually talk me into playing for two other clubs he played for, run by a character named Ted Barry, the Grosvenor and Pendleton Wednesday FC. Pendleton playing in the Manchester Wednesday league. My memories from this time are pretty vague but certain characters and events survive. To start with, Ted Barry appeared to me as a lovable rogue. Ted had a place next to Victoria station called 'The Old Vic'.

Tuff Footy

On first entering the Vic it reminded me of a picture I had of an old London pub at the turn of the century, populated by bizarre characters who looked like they were part of the fittings, not a place for a first date. But according to Ted, it made money. With black pudding the delicacy at the bar how could it fail? Ted must have been in his 50s when I first met him but give him his due, his enthusiasm never waned. To my shock more than surprise, for my first match for Wednesday although we had a full squad, Ted played himself at right full back. Now Ted at this stage of his life was far from being a fit man. Let's say a little overweight and with his trademark bandana, he looked ready for a couple of rounds with Mick McManus. But Ted was no fool, he knew the rest of his teammates were good enough and fit enough to plug the leak that seemed to be flowing through our right defensive position.

My strongest memory from my time playing for Ted came about during my second season. The Grosvenor had reached the semi final of the County Cup at Manchester's County ground. Our opponents were New Cross Celtic. A frightening prospect, the New Cross squad contained some of the let's say more forceful players who certainly made the referee earn his pennies. And if you were unlucky enough to have a weak ref when playing New Cross then without doubt you were in trouble. Players like Billy Bell, Normal Lowry, Jimmy Evans and a lad named Streety, weren't opposition to trifle with. So it was with some trepidation that we walked out from the changing rooms to the immediately comforting sight of hundreds of supporters, mostly genuine football fans determined to enjoy a lovely summer's evening watching two local clubs. The reason for our comfort being their very presence, which would surely inhibit our opponent's dubious tactics. It didn't quite work out that way. Whispered threats were the order of the day. Slightly off-putting when receiving the ball facing your own goal. We had to dig deep to compete physically with New Cross.

Most players on both sides seemed a little nervous on the ball probably because most of us hadn't played in front of such a big crowd. The tackles flew in, chances were few but the tension in the players seeped through to the crowd. The 80th minute of the match arrived with both teams still looking for a breakthrough. Their left full-back Jimmy Evans (who'd hardly given me a kick – no pun intended!) after an overhit forward pass from our captain Tommy Alan left Jimmy with the task of executing a simple pass back to his 'keeper. I decided to gamble and sprinted past Jimmy who hadn't struck the ball cleanly, my pace took me past Jimmy and within a couple of yards of the ball, their 'keeper came rushing out as I reached the ball I chipped it over the oncoming 'keeper as a roar went up even before the ball bounced into the empty net. The last 10 minutes seem to last a good hour. At least it seemed that way.

The threats grew louder and the tackles nastier as New Cross's inhibitions evaporated with the passing time. After one particularly nasty tackle on our centre forward Dave Brown at least 12 players got involved. The referee eventually restored order with the help of a handful of bookings. I've never experienced anything like that last five minutes, manic threats of bodily harm when you next touched the ball, sly digs in the ribs on the blind-side. I've played in a whole lot of rough hard games but this was different, this was bordering on hate. That final whistle was one of the sweetest sounds I've ever heard. Not too many hands were shaken and uncontrolled delight reigned with us players congratulating each other and our manager and supporters. It was a tough game where all our players had to step up to the plate and that they did, every last man. I was so proud of them. It was a great time, only slightly spoiled by the ensuing "kafuffle" that included allegations I was a contract pro and shouldn't have been allowed to play. After a meeting of the league committee, the whole fiasco was covered by the Football Pink, it was decided there was no case to answer. What a carry on.

The Alfred St. Mob

Knocking about with the Alfred Street mob was something I really enjoyed. Mick Greenacre was a funny, witty guy. Glen Fothergill was a lad you could always rely on, Sandra Derbyshire was a good time girl in the nicest sense of the phrase. And Harry Chadwick, apart from being one of the snappiest dressers I ever knew was also one of the most knowledgeable lads I knew. We never got up to much, by today's standards we were pansies. Worst thing we ever did was steal a crate of ale from the Ukrainian Club in Openshaw Street. We made our way to Inspiration Point down Gigg where we drank the lot then chatted till the early hours. Inspiration Point was a place I'd visit periodically when big decisions needed to be made. Around midnight I'd sit on its peak in the moonlight with the river Roach babbling by, it was a place conducive to deep serious thought. It worked for me. But lately things with the gang had taken a sinister twist.

That twist was drugs. They would eventually have a devastating effect on the whole gang, I say eventually because at first things changed little. I knew I was slow on the uptake but even I was surprised how long it took me to catch on and only then because of an argument. We were sat round a fire we'd made on the spare ground at the back of Mick and Harry's house on Alfred Street. We were just chatting when the subject of drugs came up. Very soon a full blown argument between Harry and Mick about who was the most knowledgeable about drugs arose. I was shocked and just blurted out "how the hell do you two know anything about drugs?" There followed an uncomfortable silence with Harry, Mick and Sandra just staring at the ground. Glen, to be fair, looked as shocked as me. As green as I was, the picture became clear. After the usual questions; when did it start, what are you taking, it turned out the three of them had been using amphetamines for around six months. But the news that hit me hardest was the news that Harry and Mick had been experimenting with heroin.

The little knowledge I possessed about heroin was sufficient for me to worry about the future. These were people I loved, I knew things would change and not for the better. My time spent with the gang would grow less and less, they became part of a world I wanted no part in. This knowledge apparently being no deterrent. Harry would hold his job down at Antlers but in the end that would come to an end.

The story is a sadly predictable one. Mick succumbed to an early death. Sandra followed suit shortly afterwards. The light at the end of the tunnel was in Harry's case. With massive effort he kicked the habit and found religion in the form of Jehovah. "God bless Jehovah." He would enjoy a good many years, marry and raise a family. But even in Harry's case his past caught up with him. He was worried, he told me he was

The 'One Arch'. Each time I approached this arch, I never failed to feel excited. I never knew for sure what lay beyond.

convinced there was something seriously wrong with his health. I told him not to worry and that only the good die young. He laughed and seemed in decent spirits, we shook hands and parted. Drugs, although Harry had been clean for many years, had done their damage. What a waste. I can't sit in judgement. I'm a smoker. I guess I just get angry at the futility of it all.

Marriage and Fatherhood

It was around 1976 when I began courting a girl I worked with called Jackie Chadwick. Jackie was a Heywood girl from a housing estate at the back of Hopwood Unionist Club. Jackie loved a giggle and had such a cute smile. It was hard not to be attracted to her. A couple of nights a week Jackie would take the bus to Bury, I would meet her at the bus stop opposite the Roach pub on Rochdale Road. Most of the night would be spent in the roach feeding the juke box, playing hits of the day. Our favourite being "Miss Grace."

It didn't matter which pub we would call in it was always the Peel for the last orders. Jackie was so happy when I told her I had wrote a poem for her. As I went to refresh our drinks I handed her the card containing the poem. It went: "We have our ups and downs like all lovers do, but you know in your heart, that I worship you. So don't ever think of setting me free for you're the only good thing that has happened to me. When I returned with our drinks Jackie's tears had been forced from their hiding place and were flowing freely. A little embarrassed at the attention we were attracting from the other regulars, we moved on to the Turf around the corner. Jackie told me she couldn't believe I had wrote her such a beautiful poem. Last orders found us in the Peel.

On returning from the loo and returning to my seat I caught Jackie just staring at me, obviously upset. "What's up Jackie, what's up?" Then it dawned, the Jim Reeves song from which I had borrowed the words for my poem was playing on the juke box. What're the bloody chances! That night ended with me escorting a reluctant Jackie to her bus stop, trying to convince her it is the thought that counts. As her bus arrived my parting words were "See you at work tomorrow". She cast me a blank look and disappeared into the night. The following day, after giving me a severe leaving alone for most of it, she finally accepted my apology and gave me a big hug to let me know all was well.

It wasn't long before Jackie fell pregnant. Our folks, once the evidence was not to be hidden, quickly organised our marriage. It took place at Bury Registry Office on Parson's Lane. Then it was back to where else but the Peel for the reception. Two weeks before the festivities my son Lee would enter the world. These weren't the days where Dads were welcomed into the delivery room. The couple of hours before, I spent in the George and Dragon facing the hospital. The landlord had built a lovely fire which was going nicely as I entered. After ordering a pint of Guinness I sat facing the fire. There's something hypnotic about staring into flames, it induces a trance-like state. As I sat there waiting for news of Jackie and the child, thoughts raced through my head too fast to settle on any one subject. Boy or girl? Would they be healthy? Jackie's sister Susan

Me and my son Lee, 1976, Oxford Street.

arrived through the pub door in an excited state. "It's a boy!" We hurried back to the maternity ward. The sight of Jackie sat up in bed with our baby cradled safely in her arms is a scene I will never forget. Emotion got the better of me. It didn't matter – there's certain times in a fella's life where it's OK to cry and this was one of them.

I gratefully accepted baby Lee into my arms to loving murmurs from the family members gathered. "You'll be alright kid" was the promise I made mentally then. And would never waiver from it. The marriage wouldn't survive but my bond with Lee would only grow stronger and friendship with his mother would last to this day, plus visits to his Nana and Grandad. The debt I owe them for their part in moulding Lee into the polite, rounded young man he is today, I could never repay.

Dancing Fool

Our parting left me feeling a little low in spirits. I made up my mind to lay low for a while, which suited my mood. A couple of uneventful months passed when my mucker, Alan Dawber came round. Alan, along with his brother Steven were cracking lads, good solid mates. To cut a long story short, before he left I'd given my word to Alan that I would go with him that following Sunday to Bury Social Club on Gigg Lane. Bury Social Club at that time was the best night to be had in Bury on a Sunday evening. Good music including live groups, decent beer and good company. Well that Sunday me and Alan went along in our glad rags and Alan, bless him, did his best to ensure I had a good night.

As pint after pint of Guinness went down, I began to get into the swing. Alan meanwhile, being a very confident fella, started chatting to two lovely-looking girls. I don't know why but this situation always made me feel awkward, somehow pretentious. Alan suggested we all have a dance. As the only dance taught to me by my brothers was the 'Kavanagh soft shoe shuffle' which basically involved shifting your weight from one foot to the other with straight arms shadowing the feet, giving the impression of someone showing someone else to a vacant seat, or even rhythmic shovelling, I had my doubts. With a lot of coaxing from Alan I took my position on the dance floor alongside Alan, facing the two girls. You know when you're dreading something, praying it won't happen, for a minute or two your mind is totally fixed on it, almost daring it to happen and speaking personally it never lets me down. The two girls started whispering then openly cracked up laughing. Well me and my embarrassment were out of there in a flash. It seemed a long lonely walk home, along Gigg Lane onto Parkhills Road and onto Heywood Street. When I finally reached home it was still early. I sat there feeling as low as a guy can get on a Saturday night. A little time passed before I realised no-one else was home.

Before I could talk myself out of it, I'd brought down the full length mirror from the bedroom, searched through my collection for a couple of dance singles, George McRae's 'Rock Ya Baby' and 'A Man Like Me' by Jimmy James. With one thought in my mind. I will learn to dance. I knew I'd never be a Travolta but I didn't really want to be, good enough to just blend in, and not stand out for the wrong reason would be good enough for me. An hour later my efforts were bearing fruit, I found that by really listening to the music I was moving smoothly and rhythmically. I got to the point where I decided to try a slow dance to a soul song. What better song than 'These Arms of Mine' by Otis Redding. The problem of my non-existent partner was filled by my niece's four foot teddy bear 'Bobby'. I held Bobby close and swooned dreamily round our living room to Otis's beautiful song.

"Eamon!" The sound of my name and knowing it wasn't me who uttered it filled me with dread. I looked sheepishly round and there stood our Kathleen and two of her mates, chips in hands, just staring at me, not uttering a word. I honestly couldn't think of a damn thing to say. So I just pardoned myself and in a sort of daze, me and Bobby made our way up the stairs to my room. Sat on my bed, head in my hands, I expected and got manic laughter making its way up the stairs to enter my ears for the second time in one night. No need to add, I didn't sleep very well. Well there's always a silver lining. The words 'fancy a dance?' no longer filled me with dread. In fact on a good night I become a dancing fool. Bury's dance floors hold no fear for me now, the Kay Club, Rebecca's, Atmosphere, Nailor's Green and Bury Social were all places I'd swing a leg if I was lucky, with a pretty lady, other times with a mate. A little awkward sure, but dancing anyway. When you're dancing the blues just float away.

My One and Only Streak

One Sunday me and the gang from work were at Bury Social Club to celebrate Mick Green's birthday. Anyone who knows Greenie knew enough to know it wouldn't be a quiet night, Mick's party trick was to stand at the bar chatting with the barmaid with his pants round his ankles, not everyone's idea of humour but it always tickled me. Well by last orders we were all a little merry. Mick, by his standards, had been fairly quiet, so it didn't come as too much of a surprise when Mick Gent came up to me and told me "Greenie" had decided we were all doing a streak from the club to Openshaw Park on Pimhole Road. We were to run in single file and Mick told me I was to be the front runner. Even as he spoke I was trying to work out the quickest, quietest route. As drunk as I was I was both excited and terrified, being naturally on the shy side, to lead a troupe of naked blokes on a run through some of Bury's more colourful streets, even at midnight filled me with dread. Well we all assembled at the side of the club and after closing time ten of us had stripped to our shoes, we made bundles of our clothes which were then clasped under our arms like rolls of wallpaper, and we were off.

As I set off there was a scream from my left side, as I looked round there was a gang of girls who were now in hysterics screaming lewd comments, very unbecoming for young ladies. Although in somewhat of a haze I knew where I was going, down Gigg Lane and up Alfred Street, right at Hurst Street, on to the park. With this in my head I took the left turn leading the troupe onto Alfred Street. A quick glance informed me as a group we were still intact, apart from a couple of stutters allowing for a couple of the crew to throw up. We were making good progress. Brilliant.

I could see to the top of the hill on Alfred Street that formed the railway bridge for the Bury Heywood line and to my delight there was not a soul in sight. My joy was short lived as we made the crest of the hill. I was engulfed in the headlights of a slow moving police car. I turned round to see the others making speedy exits down the railway embankment. I felt like a rabbit caught in lamplight, waiting for a bang on the head. Unconsciousness at this moment felt almost welcome. Luckily the survival instinct kicked in and I was off like Billy Whizz. I covered the short distance to Wood Street Mill on James Street in a flash. I was over the fence and heading for Inspiration Point. As the police torch light from James Street became a dot in the night I relaxed a little, as I made the train tracks I heard voices. Keeping myself hidden to make sure it was only the streak gang. No need for caution, it was the lads. We all made our way to the point, where we had a good laugh about our high jinks. The escapade seemed to have had a sobering effect on all the lads. We all agreed it was an invigorating exercise, very liberating and without a doubt left us all feeling not a little giddy. We must have stayed on the point a good hour, with work in the morning reluctantly we made our way home, fully dressed. I was woken in the morning by Mum shouting that I was late for work.

Arriving in work an hour late I couldn't help but notice many of my workmates sniggering in my direction. I assumed word had got round of our midnight escapade. When dinner break arrived I got a cup of tea and my lunch and took my usual seat amongst my usual dinner break gang. One of the lads called Craig asked me "is it true then?" "Is what true?" "What we've been told?" Well, what have you been told? I asked. "We were told you led a gang of streakers up Alfred Street last night. You were seen by the police before you made your escape. The police have made a statement saying they have a description of the front-man. But have decided not to pursue the case for lack of evidence." Greenie! I'll kill him!

Mr. Bugeja

The second incident with Johnny which upset me at the time, but later saw the funny side to it, took place a good five years after the first. I'd briefly met a girl in a pub in Radcliffe. I was out with a mate and so was she. I couldn't help but keep glancing over. She was lovely and although slow on the uptake, I sensed a little interest on her part. My mate who was with me Brian turned to me after observing the glances and said "Come on, let's get over there". Brian then rose from his seat and made his way over to where the girls were sitting. I was beside myself with embarrassment. I am useless in these situations. God knows what Brian was saying to them. The three of them seemed to be getting along just fine. I noticed Brian pointing over to me. The next thing they were all cracking up. I was sat there squirming in my seat. Then Brian shouted "Come on you girl". I could willingly have slugged him for that comment. With no options left I rose from my seat to join them with quite a bit of colour in my cheeks. Brian found it all very amusing (confident bugger).

After being introduced to Julie and the lovely Joanne, who insisted I call her Jo, gradually the feeling of being a prize wally subsided. In all, we were only together for around 40 minutes but I was smitten. It turns out Julie and Jo were on the way to join some friends for a girls night out. Their final destination was the Farmers Arms by the side of Elton Res. As Julie and Jo got up to go Jo with her left hand on my shoulder gave me a light peck on my cheek. I thought at that moment I could have died a happy man. Brian was looking at me and laughing. "Go and ask her if you can see her again". I didn't need telling twice. I was out the door shouting her name. I caught up with her and Julie as they made their way to the Boar's Head to meet the other girls. Julie very tactfully said "I'll get the drinks" and wandered off.

Then came one of those bittersweet moments. After asking her if she'd meet me the following Saturday in the Royal, Silver Street, Bury, there was a brief moment when she looked into my eyes and I feared the worst. Then she smiled and said "so it's not true what you're mate says then?" I just looked at her, gormless. "Forget it, see you next Saturday," she said. I don't remember too much about returning to the Ram's Head, I honestly think I was floating. Although feeling mighty fine, I needed to know what Brian had said about me to Jo. Before I'd joined them, Brian seemed a little evasive. Until he knew I wouldn't let it go. He then said "Oh! It was nothing, just something like 'at times I'm sure he's queer' all he wants to do is play football." Cheers Brian.

It's a wonder she agreed to meet me. And meet me she did and at the allotted time, my God what a vision, she looked stunning. A pair of jeans which looked like she was poured into them, a short black jacket over a coloured lacy top. Wow! With her auburn hair tumbling over her shoulders, she looked perfect. I meanwhile was resplendent in a pair of checked trousers, platform shoes, a yellow cheesecloth shirt (no collar) all finished off with my dark blue velvet jacket. Yes, I know. In spite of the way I was dressed, Jo seemed to me, during the course of the night, to be really enjoying herself. On the occasions we came across anyone I knew I begrudgingly introduced Jo and was glad when they went on their way. We agreed to end the night with a trip to the Bury centre nightclub Rebecca's. To gain entry to this nightclub it was necessary to descend a long flight of stairs. On reaching the bottom of the stairs where I paid mine and Jo's entry fee I heard my name shouted aloud and turned round to find my old mate "Johnny Begeja." What followed was perhaps the most unreal sequence of events I've ever been involved with.

Johnny grabbed the back of my hair with his clenched left hand while pulling me backwards his right hand holding me to him while he kissed me full on the lips for what seemed a good 20 seconds, Now you may think: why didn't you break free? But remember this was a night I'd drunk a lot of ale, partly because I was nervous, and would anyone expect what happened? Anyway Johnny eventually let me go as all around him our communal mates were in bits laughing. What could I say? I just stood there shaking my head, thinking how crazy is this man? Eventually I gathered my senses, then realised Jo was nowhere to be seen. After rushing out of the club through Millgate I caught her as she was getting into a taxi at Kay Gardens. After pleading with her to step out of the taxi so I could explain about Johnny Bugeja's quirky sense of humour, she placed what was to be our final kiss on my lips. Jo made me promise to not come looking for her. Reluctantly I agreed. We hugged and she vanished into the night. I was desolate and cried all the way home. It would be a good while before I could look back and laugh about these events. But, looking back over them, I could definitely understand Jo's actions. But I was so tempted to break my promise of not looking for her.

Religion vs Football

Whilst my Saturdays were taken up giving my all for Huntly FC my team mate Brian Wilcox (Snowy) asked if I would be interested in joining him and his team mates at Duke William FC in the Bury Sunday league. I asked Snowy to let me think about it. There was a reason for my hesitance. Church! At this time I was still a practicing Catholic, although a slightly disillusioned one. For several years I had been helping out at St Maries doing minor chores like running errands, cleaning and giving out prayer books. Well a decision had to be made. My love of football or my spiritual well-being. A few days later around midnight found me – where else? In the tranquillity of that place. I don't know! Nearer my God to thee, whatever it was. I whispered a request for a sign, any sign. A shooting star, "will o' the wisp" by the river bank, a moth landing on me, anything out of the ordinary. Alas it wasn't to be. At this time in my life the selfish me won out. I informed Snowy of my decision.

Duke William were a decent side. We caused a few upsets but, if I'm honest, we were never going to set the world on fire. If I'm honest, after our home games at Ainsworth Hall Road us players would make our way along Bury Old Road to the lovely old pub where we would sit around in cosy surroundings to dissect our performance that day. A few hours later we'd head to our respective homes, won or lost, we were happy.

The Bury Sunday League at that time had in its ranks some very strong teams. Cricketers FC. Thrush FC. Swan & Cemetery and top of the heap; Raven FC. Their manager, Walter Duckworth (Ducky) the sort of bloke you tended to agree with a lot, had gathered around him the cream of Bury's football talent. Players like Pete Locky, Bob Barras, Ian McCool, Brian Green, Alan Whitehead who went on to play for Bury FC. Hutchi and, in my opinion, the finest amateur player in my lifetime, Dave Wolfenden. Standing around 5'11" slim as a latte, instant control, like a feline predator lurking on his favoured left wing, he would approach the defender at speed and cleverly tempt him by showing just enough of the ball, just enough for him to commit himself. With speed that defied belief the ball would be pushed past him and over a short distance you weren't going to catch 'Wolfy'. He would hit the byline and more often than not his crosses would cause chaos in the opposing defence. On other occasions he'd cut inside and unleash shots that the opposing 'keeper seemed reluctant to get in the way of.

I always enjoyed watching David, I'd go as far as to say I'd pay good money for the privilege. Wolfy in his day was a joy to behold. At that time any team who came away from a meeting with Walt Ducky's Raven with anything more than a good hiding would be well happy. It would be a few years later before I would be playing in a Peel FC side that would give Raven a sound beating.

Shopping With Mum

On the rare occasions I'd accompany Mum on a shopping trip, one place we always went was Chadwick's black pudding stall. Mum loved them. I had to smother mine in French mustard – lovely! Mum was a rummager. These were the days before charity shops (of which I'm a regular patron.) We'd seek out the second hand stalls on the old Bury outside market.

The old inside market was brilliant, it had an atmosphere all of its own. Me and Mum would take time out for a cup of tea and a cake at Redmond's cafe. While still a kid, it was with Mum shopping on the market that I experienced my first and only, total eclipse. I honestly thought it was the end of the world. Even with Mum's reassurance I wasn't convinced. The abattoir at the Art Picturehouse end of the market was a place I'd delivered papers to, I used to sprint the 100 or so yards to the letter box as some of the sights I'd rather not see. After our shopping trip Mum would insist on taking a long cut home that would mean walking to Moorgate to Porrits shop where Mum would come away with a rabbit or, if Dad had some overtime, some nice fish pieces. I once saw a picture of Porrits shop with the whole shop front up to the roof covered in rabbits. It was a rare old sight. Porrits, if I'm right, was the last of the old shops to hold out until alas even that went under the bulldozer. Whether the giant impersonal buildings being erected now will be an improvement, time will be the judge.

Brian Joins the Ratting Club

Brian up to now showed no interest in hunting the rat. Reckoned he had enough trouble with the two-legged variety. After attempting to entice him with tales of the stealth and skill involved, and if he didn't think he was up to it I would understand. Like a red rag to a bull. Sure enough one warm summer evening Brian joined me toting his brand new air rifle and a definite air of the hunter. With Percy my ferret up my jumper, probably asleep, and Tina my dog at my side we set off for the banks of the Roach in pursuit of the rat.

Most of the time was taken up with rummaging through the vegetation along the Roach's bank, the time to get excited was when Tina had her nose to a hole with her tail wagging. This would be the cue for Percy to do his stuff. Percy wore a small brass bell round his neck. This little bell would serve two purposes; the first was the noise of the bell as Percy made his way down the dark tunnel would give the occupants a chance to escape through the bolt hole. There was always a bolt hole and usually more than one. The second purpose was, after the rifles and Tina had done their work and things had calmed down, it would be Tina's job to listen and locate Percy's whereabouts. We would then move on, keeping a close eye on Tina's rear end, hoping for a wag. This would go on; covering great distances, sometimes stretching from the Seven Arches to Goshen playing fields, no wonder we never put any weight on.

One night Brian phoned me in an excited state informing me he'd bought a puppy, a Jack Russell, the same breed as Tina. I went straight round to Bry's, I found the whole family jostling each other for a hold of the new family member. Bry informed me the puppy's name was 'Snowy'. When Snowy reached the right age she would join us on her first hunt. Bry was thinking along the lines of Snowy taking a lead from Tina's example, which to me seemed fair enough. That evening would prove to be Snowy's Waterloo. After marking a hole just before we hit Heap Bridge, Percy had been down the hole less than ten seconds when all hell broke loose.

There were rats everywhere. There was one huge specimen came bounding out of a bolt-hole a foot to the side of Snowy. Instinct ensued on both sides, Snowy was on the rat in a flash. She held the rat in her jaws. Snowy's youth let her down here; an experienced dog in this situation would shake the rodent vigorously. Snowy's passive grip allowed the rodent to twist round and inflict a vicious bite. This had the effect of Snowy releasing the rat with a high pitched yelp before making off like a scalded cat. With Bry's shouts of "Snowy come back here now" falling on deaf ears we had no option but to collect Percy from the bank and set out to find her. With Tina leading the search we were confident we'd soon have her back.

This scene shows our favourite ratting territory, with Antler's Pilot Mill dominating the scene.

Alas even with Tina's keen senses our search would prove fruitless so reluctantly we made our way home. I'd only been home a few minutes, halfway through making a brew after putting Percy back in his hutch with his favourite treat, a piece of liver, when the phone rang. It was Bry telling me that, when he got to his house, Snowy was waiting sheepishly in the garden. Nothing wrong with her tracking ability then. Me and Bry persevered with Snowy but it soon became obvious she was never going to make a ratter, whether it was the incident with the rat or just plain old disinterest. Who knows.

Before long Snowy would be laid up with half a dozen lovely half breed puppies, the father preferring to remain anonymous. The bottom drawer containing the puppies was placed in the opposite corner to the telly in the living room of Bry's Heywood Street home. Weeks passed and the pups were thriving. Bry genuinely loved Snowy even with her shortcomings in the ratting department. Tragedy would strike in the form of a fire in Bry's living room, started, we think, accidentally by young Clifford and a couple of his little mates. The fire caught hold and the room was gutted. Needless to say poor Snowy and the puppies perished. Bry was devastated and for a while it was a case of tiptoeing round him.

When I sensed the memory was less raw I suggested we call at The Roach for a couple of pints and maybe a game of arrows. Bry half-heartedly agreed. That evening I called for Bry, my knock on the door was answered by his gorgeous older sister Dolores. "Brian's not playing out today" she said, then cracked up laughing. I just stared at her, lost in the vision. She must have thought "what a gawp". We passed the gutted living room then into the back room where most of the family members were gathered. "Brian's upstairs getting ready, won't be long" said Mrs. Heys. I was in no rush for him to come down. Dolores was ironing a small pile of clothes. With me thinking "it's a lucky guy who ends up with her" I was fetched back to earth as Bry's voice broke in. "Ready Eam." We bid farewell and made our way to the welcoming atmosphere of The Roach pub.

On our way in, there were two lads sat on the bench outside, one I recognised as Baz Cookson, an acquaintance of mine and Bry's. "Alright Baz?" "Alright Eamon?" Strange, no greeting between Baz and Brian. As we sat down with our pints I asked Bry if there was a problem between him and Baz. Bry said it was nothing. I thought to myself the chances were that 'nothing' would include a girl. Bry was a bit quiet which I expected so I was prepared to do all the talking. No hardship I assure you. After an hour or so Bry said he was just going to the loo. After about ten minutes, with no Bry, I knew something was up. I called into the gents, no sign.

As I was on my way out I heard a commotion. I flew out and there they were, Bry and Baz, beating the hell out of one another. I managed to get between them and with the help of Baz's mate we managed to pull them apart. As Baz was pulled one way and me pulling Bry the other, threats filling the air, order was restored. I coaxed Bry into The Peel, a regular sanctuary for stressed local folk. Our pints of Guinness were almost empty when I turned to Bry and said "Well, come on, what was that all about?" Bry explained that, on his way back from the loo Baz was at the doorway and shouted for Bry to join him a minute. Bry said that when he got up to Baz he whispered "Bry get up to Heywood Street, they're selling hot dogs outside your house." Oh, my God! No Eamon, hold yourself. God no, I couldn't help it, I just fell to bits. "Bry I'm sorry" I said as tears of laughter ran down my face. "I can't help it." Then it happened. Bry couldn't hold his poker face. He just cracked up. "You two alright?" asked Dennis the landlord. "Two more pints please Dennis" was my response. After toasting Snowy and the pups with our refreshed pints we put it all to bed.

New Pastures

There comes a time when everyone reassesses their situation. Like most folk, I thought I could do with more money. Working at Antlers was OK but the money was poor. Also I'd found myself in Alan's office once more. The firm had started importing more and more foreign suitcases from abroad, mostly Taiwan. This wasn't a good sign for the future. It wasn't too hard to imagine the mill becoming just a warehouse. The final insult as far as me and my workmate Tommy McKenzie were concerned was when a large white sign was erected over the exit door. In large bold red letters was written "Buy British".

The next day, while on overtime, with Tommy keeping watch, armed with a small tin of paint, I altered the R in British to L. I was delighted with the resulting 'Buy Blitish'. So apt for the situation. Next morning our handiwork was noticed by one of the early arrivals and before long a large group of the workforce had gathered, pointing, laughing and chatting, probably about who the culprit could be. Sure enough it wasn't long before I was sat facing Alan in the privacy of his office.

"Well Eamon I've no proof it was you. So I'm asking you, man to man, was it?" Don't ask me why. I don't know why. But I admitted to Alan it was me. I also told him my reasons, and I honestly felt justified. Alan just stared at me for what seemed ages, then said "Eamon I can't keep letting you get away with your childish pranks."

Now get this. I said to Alan "Sack me". "Have you seen the Bury Times today? There's a dozen jobs I could go for this afternoon." Happy days. Again Alan just stared at me (God bless him.) I honestly think he had no idea what to say. In the end I had to say something. I got up from my chair, offered Alan my hand, which he accepted and shook, looking puzzled. "Don't worry Al" I said, "you won't have to put up with me much longer." Alan finally said "Don't do anything rash Eamon." "I won't."

Well I'd done it – I'd forced my own hand. I'd put myself in a position where now I had to find another job. A couple of weeks later I was bidding goodbye to my Antler workmates, followed by comments like "He'll soon be back". Did they know something I didn't? The following Monday I was saying hello to my new workmates at Bury's famous toffee factory 'Bensons'.

Not so sweet at Bensons

Bensons was similar to Antlers in as much as it was a place nearly every other person in Bury at one time or another had worked. I arrived bright and early and prepared for anything. Just as well. On being introduced to a fella called Lee who was to be my foreman he seemed a nice fella, easygoing, and he spent an hour or so with me explaining the practicalities of the job I'd been assigned to. I was to work in the C room.

My workbench had a square stainless steel top about five foot by five foot, with an inch deep stainless steel rimmed container, filled with various flavoured liquids stocked on a raised shelf above the bench. Today I'd be working with lemon. Lee showed me, after mixing the liquid in a metal bucket containing red hot toffee how to pour it onto the steel bench where it would immediately begin to cool. The crux of the job was timing. As the cooling toffee reached the required texture, I was to cut it into manageable pieces with a pair of scissors. Yes, a pair of scissors. Success rested on the toffee being just the right texture. The toffee I prepared was to be fed into a machine that moulded it into bite sized pieces and then wrapped them in toffee paper. But, and in my case it was a big but, if the prepared toffee was too hard it would jam the machine, if too soft, the same thing, but a messier result. It took awhile and a few rows with Margaret, the Scottish girl operating the machine I was feeding but eventually I became capable. I knew from the start Bensons wasn't to be my Eldorado but it would do for now.

There happened to be a couple of old mates serving time at Bensons at the time I was there. Damian Faddiack (Damo!) a lad whose company I always enjoyed and a lad called Tony Lomax who I'd already worked with at Antlers. My strongest memory of Tony was of me and him sat in my house at Raby Street, a house I had once shared with Jackie my ex-wife, listening to Mike Hardings album "Mrs. Harding's Kid." From start to finish me and Tony were howling with laughter at Harding's stories of a Lancashire lad's hilarious takes on life, matrimonial strife and characters like Spotty Bum McGrew and Dangerous Albert. Brilliant. In reality my time at Bensons would be shorter than even I was planning.

Around five weeks into my employment there I was informed by one of my co-workers that workers were allowed to take a few toffees home as long as you didn't take liberties. One Friday I was on my way out after clocking off when this giant of a man called Fred asked me if I had any toffees on me. I answered "yes" and Fred's face seemed to lose all its colour. Fred gathered himself and asked me to follow him. He took me to a clear windowed office facing the clocking station. Embarrassing or what!

The folks queuing to clock out were all staring at me as my foreman Lee joined me and Fred. Fred informed Lee of what had passed. Lee turned to me and asked me to turn out my pockets. On doing so the contents were laid bare for all to see. Amongst my white mouse and ball of string were about four mint toffees covered in fluff. Lee took one look at my stash and said "is that it? I answered yes and he said to forget it, he'd see me on Monday. I thanked Lee for his leniency but knew there and then I wouldn't be back. In my head I knew I couldn't face going back.

Not You Again

"Hi Alan, it's Eamon."

"See you on Monday Eamon."

That was the entire conversation that would see me return like a homing pigeon to the inner sanctum of the Antler Mill once again. I'd enjoyed my little sojourn but there was something about Antlers, apart from the girls, I just can't think what. Could it be the 'push penny' games at break times, the fact that I could play Johnny Cash records all day long, maybe being stood on one leg four hours a day, who knows. But this time I knew I had to keep my head down because I knew if I left again there'd be no going back.

Things improved when my mucker Bry became a workmate. The days passed quicker with Bry about. When the weather was good there was always plenty to do on the banks of the Roach, hunting with Sid Colson. Some nights, because Bry wanted to improve at football, we'd set off for the subway at the top of Spring Street that takes you on to the market. We'd get there for about 7.30pm, it was always deserted and we were rarely interrupted. With Bry at one end and me at the other whacking the ball with all our might trying to score past one another, it was great sport. No fagging the ball as there were tall walls at each end. Sometimes we'd still be there at 10pm. Bry wasn't a natural footballer but as I told him, I knew a lot of lads who weren't natural footballers but I never enjoyed playing against them. The reason being they worked harder to achieve what would come easy to a natural footballer. These were lads whose determination and effort made them worthy adversaries indeed. Bry just gave one of his looks. I knew better than to carry on. But he was improving.

Sometimes my old mate Kenny Bellis would call me to see if I fancied a kick about. We'd either go to Rocky Road park or the green off Lever Street in Radcliffe near Radcliffe Borough's ground. Now Kenny Bellis was a natural footballer and a great athlete. On the few occasions I played against Kenny I rarely enjoyed myself, he was a bloody good fullback. Sometimes after hitting 40 good passes to one another for a while we'd then play attack and defence where Kenny would invite me to try and get past him with the ball, Kenny's reasoning being that with him being a defender and me a forward it would do us both good. It struck me that this was the same thing me and my school pal Paddy Holmes used as our training for the school team. Now to me it must have been easier in the old days, fullbacks used to be big heavy bruisers who used to kick lumps out of you but weren't the most mobile of beasts. But when we come to my generation we have fullbacks like Kenny Bellis, Graham Rostron (Rossy) Mick Kavanagh, Kenny Jones, athletes all of them. What's the world coming to when you've got fullbacks as fast and nimble as wingers? Give me an overweight, cumbersome clogger every time. Me and Kenny ended up teaming up on at least three occasions with Duke William, Radcliffe Borough and then Elton Fold.

Kenny was a heart player, I loved heart players, even if they were my opponents, you might not like them but you have to respect them, even grudgingly. One of the finest examples of a heart player was Steve Burton who wrote for the Star Newspaper. It wouldn't surprise me that hardly anyone reading this had heard of Steve. But ask any lad who had the good fortune to play alongside him in the early Roach FC teams what they thought of Steve Burton. What a player. Again not a naturally gifted player. The lad just wouldn't lay down, he never knew when he was beat, if he'd been a boxer he'd have been Rocky Marciano – he never knew when to go down.

An incident that summed him up happened when we were playing the Rose and Crown from Ramsbottom on our pitch under the one Arch down Pimhole. It was the quarter final of the Yorkshire Bank Trophy. We were leading 1–0 with about five minutes to go. Steve was sprinting after their right winger when he pulled up like he'd been hit by a sniper bullet, then collapsed in a heap by the dead ball line around 10 yards from the goal post. All old footballers will immediately recognise this as a classic pulled hamstring. And nobody forgets a pulled hamstring.

The game carried on as Mick Green one of our defenders cleared the ball deep into Rose and Crown's half, instinctively the whole of our defence moved up to the halfway line. There was then a ball launched high from their six yard box that floated over the heads of our pushed up defenders which their pacey forward Paul Ryder was on to. Our 'keeper, Pete (The Tank) saw the danger and flew, well flew might be a bit strong. He rushed out to the edge of his box. Upon which young Mr. Ryder lifted the ball sweetly over Tank's head, the ball rolling towards the empty net. When Steve, who'd been down while play was going on, got to his feet and covered the ground at pace to clear the ball off the line, only for him to collapse in obvious pain again. We held out for our 1–0 win. After he was strapped up a couple of us teammates were proud to carry him back to the pig farm which was our temporary home at that time. Steve Burton to me was the quintessential 'Iron Man' and a lovely fella to boot.

Pat's First Managerial Position

Our Pat lived and breathed football. I've seen the girlfriends of lads in our local, on catching sight of our Pat entering the pub, drag their men to the next pub, rather than put up with chat all night about football, football, football. As much as I loved my football, I'd try to steer him on to other subjects, very rarely succeeding.

Pat was happiest when discussing the finer points of the beautiful game. No-one ever described Pat as a great footballer but his enthusiasm and effort were unquestioned. You could spot Pat a mile off. While he was a small fella, his beetroot red face you couldn't miss. One day I asked Pat to accompany me on a little trip in order to seek his opinion. We took a walk down Pimhole Road, past St. Thomas's school, the pig farm and under the one Arch, hard left up to the top of Inspiration Point. Once at the top I sat down on the side overlooking the river Roach and in the distance Water Farm. I patted the ground next to me and, warily, Pat took his seat. As we sat there Pat says "Well, what are we here for?" I said well, to begin with, how many times have the lads in The Roach pub and The Peel told you we should form our own team? Pat agreed there was quite a few. He also agreed among them were some damn good players. "It's not that easy Eam. There's kit, league fees and no guarantee we would be allocated a pitch," he said. "That's why you're here Pat" I told him. "Look down below. Below the railway embankment we were sat on beyond the railway sleepers that formed its border lay a field that stretched around 200 yards to the river bank and lengthways, around 300 yards, the grass although overgrown, could not conceal a very even surface. Pat looked doubtful but behind the doubt I noticed something stirring. Could it be? Yes it was there.

The smile came involuntarily to Pat's face. Before he could protest at the problems we faced I informed him I'd already had a word with the farmer, who, for a nominal fee, would let us have the field for one season. "And Pat, with you as manager how can we go wrong?" I asked him. I could feel him warming to the task. The previous season had just ended but even so there would be no time to spare. All able bodied men and boys were enlisted for the task of making a dream come true, if only for one season. During the following months we were to beg, steal or borrow to achieve this end.

One night me, our Pat and our Michael, who was home on leave from the navy, took a trip down to view our progress. We couldn't believe our eyes. It looked fantastic, half a dozen of our prospective players were busying themselves putting the finishing touches to create a site. That, I can honestly say, thrilled the three of us. From our vantage place on Inspiration Point the scene below us took some taking in. We just kept looking at each other and grinning like Cheshire cats. As we made our way down to the pitch and joined the others the chat was all positive. The future for the pitch under the one Arch was looking rosy.

One of the lads, Mick Brooks had even fitted the metal inserts that would accommodate the goalposts. As someone mentioned the goalposts we all just looked at one another. Goalposts! One of the lad's mates in Heywood had promised us a pair of goalposts that had been abandoned on some derelict land at Darn Hill, he'd phoned a couple of nights before to say when he went to collect them they'd gone. Oh my God. How the hell are we going to get a pair of goalposts? Where do you get goalposts, if we knew where to get them how could we afford them? Glum is the word to describe the mood. Our Pat who had a little money saved was more than willing to make sure the farmer got his money, after that a pair of football nets were a pipe dream.

The thing was the following week we'd arranged a friendly against crack local outfit Cricketers FC. Out of the blue one of the lads, Chris Brooks, Mick's brother, got to his feet, turned to face the rest of us and said "they'll be here tomorrow" and promptly walked off. In unison we all turned and stared at his brother Mick, hoping for a clue as to what Chris meant. Mick, in his brother's defence said "if our kid says they'll be here tomorrow they'll be here tomorrow." We all looked around us at what was looking now a mighty fine pitch. The eight of us that were left decided we'd retire to the comfort of the Roach pub to discuss our future and for one thing what to call ourselves. It's amazing how a few beers can affect your optimism. By the end of that night we'd not

Taken from 'Inspiration Point' with the River Roach in the background. In the foreground is the field that me and Pat had the idea of turning into a football pitch, which we did.

only found our name (Roach FC) but our Michael came out with one of his great understatements. "Roach FC will rise like a trout to become very well known round Bury especially down Rochdale Road."

"Now ease up there Michael!"

The next day after my tea I took Tina my Jack Russell dog down the Roach for a run and to check the pitch. I couldn't believe it. I would never doubt Chris Brooks again, true to his word he'd not only got us a pair of goalposts, they were up and running, well maybe not running but they were up. God bless him. If he'd have been in front of me I'd have given him a big sloppy kiss. What a guy.

When I returned home I told our Pat the news. "You're joking" he said. Finally convinced, Pat was on the phone to Chris. After a shorter than expected conversation our Pat replaced the receiver with a puzzled expression and just stared at the floor. "Well, what's he said?" "I asked him where he got them. He said he'd borrowed them off someone he didn't know right well." Our Pat's face was a picture. You have to understand Pat was a practicing Christian, this is a guy who in later years, after accidentally spilling paint on his carpet and on receiving the cheque from his insurers, returned it with a note saying he only needed half that amount! I kid you not.

So here was a dilemma for Pat. That following Sunday we were due to play Cricketers FC. I explained to Pat there was no time to do anything now but I would find out where Chris acquired the goalposts. This seemed to appease Pat and we turned our attention to the somewhat daunting task of how to defeat the mighty Cricketers. We had training arranged for Wednesday evening at Rocky Road park. The team would be selected from those present. There was no doubt about it, our Pat had some good young raw talent at his disposal. One young kid, Mick Williams, was a dead ringer for Brains out of Thunderbirds. Mick sure didn't look like a footballer. The horn-rimmed national health glasses not exactly helping his cause. But make no mistake, the expression 'looks can be deceiving' could have been written for this lad. The lad had class, an uncut diamond that would eventually become a perfect gem. But not just yet.

On board also were the Brooks brothers, as different as could be. Mick was tall and slender, ran with the grace of a gazelle and struck a ball as sweetly as any player I've seen. Chris was stockier and what he lacked in craft he made up for with sheer tenacity. The only player anything like Chris on the Roach's books was Carl Suthurst a little more controlled than Chris but definitely the same mould. Roy Grundy was to marshal the back four which would include our Pat and Mick Green, a small but feisty customer.

The midfield dynamo was Ste Burton. Few things you can rely on, the sun to rise each morning and Ste Burton never to back out of a tackle and myself on the right wing doing my bit for the cause. Between the sticks Pete the Tank – fastest man over ten pints. Roy Grundy, a central defender, was Mr. Reliable. What I liked about Roy was, if he could, he'd always give you the easy ball. As an out and out winger I was reliant on other players, mainly midfielders to fetch me into the game. As already quoted, I loved receiving a ball with just the full back facing me, in my gut I knew I could with either pace or trickery get behind most fullbacks. The only thing I needed to improve on was my final ball, too often head down I'd hit a hopeful ball across the goalmouth instead of a quick look up then pick someone out. This would come with time (too much time I think!) So it wasn't without a little hope we would entertain our illustrious visitors the following Sunday.

Don't ask me how but because of some argument with the then landlord of the Roach pub, we found ourselves, along with our opponents Cricketers FC getting changed in the top room of the Turf pub round the corner on Wash Lane. Not that getting changed at The Roach would have been much better, given the short distance between the two. The trip from the Turf meant we would walk (most players with their boots on) the distance to Rochdale Road, through the park and another half mile or so down Pimhole Road. None of that could take away from the excitement of the occasion.

Our first ever match on our self made pitch against one of the top sides Bury amateur football has ever produced. The excitement was tangible. I always had a healthy respect for talented opponents (sometimes, I think, too much) but our opponents that day had several players who didn't seek respect, they demanded it. Tony Holt's talents I was no stranger to, he would always occupy a place of high respect in my mind from my memories of playing alongside him as members of what I'd still consider a dream team.   That team represented St. Gabriel's school for four fabulous years alongside players like Nello and Ged McLoughlin. Tony had nifty footwork and blistering pace, a truly great player. Another player I'd heard great things about was Tich Heaton his partner in defence I knew well enough Ian McCool. I'd already played alongside his older brother Barry McCool, one of life's real characters. Ian was in the year below me at Gabriels and had earned himself a reputation as a real classy player.

But although these lads were a force to be reckoned with, the hushed whispers were reserved for a player who in a lot of local people's minds (including mine) was the best amateur player Bury's ever produced. Dave Wolfenden (Wolfy). At this time I'd only heard stories of this fella but had never seen him in the flesh. He didn't look anything special, my sneaky glances revealed, if anything he was skinny, almost frail looking. Strange when faced with big reputations we'll hope to find any kind of weakness. When playing against such opponents I'd find I would have a mixture of fear, excitement and determination. That Sunday morning I think fear got the better of a few of the Roach lads. We were given a lesson in how to play the beautiful game. Our high hopes were laid to rest as the well oiled machine ran us ragged.

They were a joy to watch. Our two fullbacks Mick Green and our Pat each in turn had to face Tony Holt or Wolfy. On the other hand the fact that we would celebrate winning a corner as the other teams celebrate a winning goal tells its own story. After their seventh goal they must have felt a little pity when in my mind they gave away a deliberate penalty. It was decided our man for the occasion would be Chris Brooks. As I've said already Chris wasn't a natural footballer but he'd run through a brick wall for you. And although to little effect today, he'd done just that. The ball was placed on the spot. Mick Forest looked a giant between the sticks, the handful of pub regulars who formed our fan club held their breaths as our hero took several steps back. He began his run and disaster struck almost immediately. Chris tripped, fell headlong and actually headed the ball on the penalty spot. At the same time big Mick Forrest collapsed in hysterics in a heap on the left of his goal as the ball came rolling past him. Mick merely pointed a finger and fell into hysterics once more.

It was a fitting end to a football match us Roach lads hopefully would learn from. I certainly learned from Wolfy that morning. He was only facing our Pat or Mick Green but although not the best in the world they were no mugs. Even so to watch the way Wolfy would tempt the defender by just sharing enough of the ball to convince them they could nick It and at the moment they chanced their luck the ball would be whisked away at lightning speed. On the rare occasions a player managed to keep alongside him, for a guy with nothing on his frame he had tremendous body strength, once past his man and this set him apart from the rest, nine times out of ten he'd find a man. He was rarely content to let fly a hopeful ball. We all learned that morning a hard lesson. But also we'd witnessed a master at work.

In years to come I'd play with and against David. I find it incredible he didn't make it as a pro. He's certainly better than most of the players I've paid to watch and, as I tell everyone, when Wolfy's name comes up, in his heyday I'd have paid to watch him. We spent a full season entertaining local teams from the Bury Sunday League, we were involved in some bloody good games and overall gave a good account of ourselves. It was lovely to see young inexperienced players maturing and acquiring the necessary skills, a few exceptionally so. They were a good bunch of lads who enjoyed each other's company on and off the field. This helped in many ways.

After each match we'd get together in the Roach. (Our Pat had sorted out the quarrel with the landlord.) And whether we'd won or lost the proceedings were always upbeat and enjoyable. We all agreed we could accept defeat if we'd given our all, to be sat in the pub after a defeat with energy to burn your pint wouldn't taste as good and that feeling that you'd done your best was not to be achieved. After several home matches the folk who owned the pig farm on Pimhole Road stopped a couple of us players and enquired about what the team was called and where we got changed. We explained we were Roach FC and we changed in the top room of our namesake. Joan and Paul as they were called, kindly offered us the use of a quite large almost empty utility room at the rear of the farmhouse. We readily accepted and thanked them. This was heaven sent as it would save the somewhat arduous journey from the Roach in our footy boots. The thing was I can't remember any of our opponents that season moaning about the trek to the pitch. As the season came to a close the farmer who owned the field said he'd be needing it the following year.

But the pitch under the Arch had served its purpose, our Pat had cut his managerial teeth and although our trophy cabinet was awaiting its first acquisition we'd really enjoyed the season and were determined to stay together and improve together. And I can definitely say that came to pass.

The Exorcist

What is it about scary films? We'll actually pay good money to watch a film that will terrify us? Everyone was talking about a film doing the rounds that was apparently loosely based on a guy who worked on the Royal Yacht Britannia. So I'm thinking, how scary can that be? The film was 'The Exorcist' and, as at that time it wasn't being shown in Bury, me and two mates from work, Bry Heys and Big Mick Suthurst made our way to Manchester.

On our way into the cinema, there were people giving out leaflets containing phone numbers to ring if the film had an adverse effect on you. That was enough for me. I told Bry and Mick I'd wait in the pub round the corner where they could meet me when the film had finished. They weren't having any of it. I was told in no uncertain terms I was going in. Under protest I took my place in the cinema, sandwiched between Mick and Bry. We sat there with the two of them trying to reassure me. "It's only a film, it's not real." But as the film started they both fell silent, while their faces revealed their confidence had vanished. I wriggled out of my Wrangler jacket and watched the less frightening parts of the film from behind it's collar.

On the train back to Bury we all agreed it was the most frightening film any of us had seen. When we reached Bury we headed straight for the Royal on Silver Street. We needed a drink. It was still quite early when I arrived at my door in Oxford Street. I'd no need of a key, the lock on the front door was only a lock in name, as I walked down the hallway the large picture of the Sacred Heart halfway down the hall was a comfort after the scenes I'd seen that night. That was to be my only comfort. No-one was home. Mum was at work at Robinson Kay home, Dad was at the pub but where was everyone else? Nine people lived in our house and not one home.

I climbed the stairs, after calling in the bathroom I passed Pat's gloomy room, made my way along the corridor that led to the girls and Michael's rooms. Turned left just before their door to the short corridor that led to mine and John's room. I hated this corridor, it just had a bad feel, even my dog Tina wouldn't tread these boards. After switching on the light I sat on John's empty bed while I undressed, my bed was pushed right up against the far wall lengthways. Once undressed I switched off the light on the wall at the side of the door. I think I was in bed before the room went dark. I held the covers over my head, till eventually I had to come up for air, facing the wall I just stared at the darkness till slowly but surely, as my eyes became accustomed to the dark, a pair of eyes began staring back at me and between the eyes a crucifix slowly appeared. I was out of that bed as quick as I'd got in, heart racing I switched on the light, nervously I made my way to the far wall.

I couldn't believe it, the spectral eyes and crucifix I thought I'd seen were there in solid fluorescent paint. I couldn't help smiling. Our John knew I was going to watch The Exorcist. What a wicked sense of humour. Years later at family get-togethers my family informed me the small corridor leading to my room was haunted. Why they hadn't told me, I can only guess.

Hargreaves

One afternoon I was walking down Lord Street and was just about to pass the office of Henry Hargreaves when I stopped and thought: why not? Go for it. Any hesitation lay in the fact that I possessed no trade and no skills, just a willing pair of hands. My sense of adventure took over any doubts and I entered the office building. There was a lady sitting at a desk as I entered. She asked me my business and I informed her I'd come in the hope of acquiring a job. She made a short phone call and I was told someone would come to see me shortly.

That someone was a lovely Scottish fella called Bill Smith (Whispering Bill.) Bill was a very softly spoken fella who asked me to follow him into a side office. He took down the necessary details. The chat then became more general, after talking for a short while I knew I was in the company of a smashing, fair minded fella. Finally Bill said "well Mr. Kavanagh, you have a position with the Erection Gang. Stifling a smile I said thank you very much. Bill informed me I would be working in Bootle in Liverpool on the Inland Revenue building. A building, I was informed, that had a place in the Guinness Book of Records on account of the amount of stoppages there. 'Scouse militancy'. Well known throughout the kingdom. I rose from my seat to shake hands with Bill and thanked him.

As I left the office and headed for the exit I heard someone say 'Eamon' – I looked round and recognised Jim Sharples. Jim was a fella I'd met in my local The Peel a few times, a very agreeable chap. During our chat I informed Jim of what had just taken place with me and Bill. Jim was pleased for me and told me he was a chargehand and at the time was stationed at Bootle on the same site. Jim kindly told me he would give me a lift. We agreed a time and a place, shook hands and parted and I walked out feeling a pretty lucky fella.

So once again it was adios to my Antler workmates and into the unknown. As Jim had told me, he was only to be at Bootle a couple more days. The following Monday myself and Jim made the trip to the town of Bootle. The guy I had to report to told me my first job was to find some digs. Handing me a couple of place names and addresses I set off in search of future lodgings.

The first place I came to was dodgy to say the least. I was taken up two flights of stairs and shown to a room and told to see what I thought. The room was about twelve feet square and was dominated by a big old wardrobe that had seen better days. There was one small window which left the room dull even though I'd walked in out of bright sunshine, a shiny threadbare carpet and two single beds pushed hard up against opposite walls. There was a lad around the same age as me checking himself in the cracked mirror of the wardrobe. On my greeting of "All reet" he smiled and said in a strong Scouse accent "you're not from these parts then."

I told him I was from a small town in Lancashire called Bury. "Oh Bury! Terry McDermott, Alec Lindsay." I smiled and nodded. He then informed me if I was to take the room "that's yours" pointing to one of the single beds. The wall it was up against was covered in black mould. The lad then said "I pulled it away from the wall but the cockroaches pulled it back. As he cracked off laughing my mind was decided. I think I'll leave it. As I made my way down the stairs he shouted after me that he was only joking about the cockroaches.

Rosie's

The next address found me at the door of a gable end house in a row of neat terraced houses. The date over the door was 1890. I always had a thing about old buildings. Answering my knock stood a stout lady about '50ish wearing a nice clean apron. Speaking in a refined Liverpool accent – there is such a thing – as she looked up from my suitcase (Antlers) she said "come in, you look lost. My name's Rosie."

As I followed Rosie down the hall I was taken with the homeliness of the place and, more importantly, it was clean. Rosie showed me to the room, the only room she had spare (a good sign) and said that, whether I wanted the room or not there'd be a cup of tea waiting for me in the common room. The room was small but well lit, there was a picture on the wall over the neat bed that my Mum loved and had hanging in the hallway of her Oxford Street home. The picture was of a young girl of about seven. Attired in a lovely turn-of-the-century dress, at her side stood a lovely collie dog, the little girl rested her left hand on the dog's shoulder. That picture assured me I would be right to choose this room. I suppose I did feel like a lost boy. If I'm really honest, a little frightened and seeking assurances in any form.

I went down to inform Rosie I liked the room. On agreeing that £3 a day which included sandwiches for me to take to work and my tea, I told Rosie I'd better get off as it was my first day. As I turned to leave Rosie grabbed me by the arm, stared into my eyes and said "listen lad, you're as good as anyone." What is it, when you're feeling emotional you can be moved almost to tears by kind words. Rare people like Rosie have a sixth sense concerning matters such as this. God bless her kind.

I needed to pull myself together to face the job in hand. Arriving back at the site I sought out my chargehand, a fella called Michael, an Irish bloke who on hearing my name, made no attempt to hide his fondness of it. Michael introduced me to a Scottish lad named Chris. "Eamon you'll be Chris's mate, he'll tell you what to do."

On reaching Chris's workplace he confessed to me he'd only ever worked on ships and struggled to read maps I was stunned, what could I say? But I knew there and then the bonus which Michael had mentioned to me seemed at this moment a distant dream. Somehow Chris muddled through his working day and I muddled right behind him. Fitting ventilation ducting had its interesting points, sadly I wouldn't see much of these and, because of Chris's ignorance of the job, he made little headway. Luckily Michael, our chargehand, noticed this and asked me to do jobs to help others. One of these jobs was testing the finished line of ducting, which was a bit of a nightmare, requiring you to set up a machine at one end of the ducting to blow air under pressure through the whole line of ducting until you had a steady pressure reading. This proved to be a real task as holes were many and widespread with no indication of their location. This meant you had to find a suspect area and set your ladders up. Climb up, in this case the required 30 feet, listen and feel, and if you got lucky, block the hole with a special sealant and wearily move on to the next one. One day I spent the whole of it on one length of ducting about 40 yards long. As I sealed the last hole I genuinely expected a round of applause.

During my stay in Bootle which lasted around four months, each day after work I'd leave work feeling weary but at the same time good. The work was hard and frustrating but it was man's work (look fellas I'm a man) and then to cheer me up I had Rosie's smiling face and lovely food to go back to. It seemed to me, if we stopped paying, Rosie would just carry on anyway; she mothered us, me and the other half dozen customers residing with her. Rosie's husband Harry had been taken by the big C a couple of years before. Sometimes, on the couple of occasions I did not go home to Bury at the weekend I'd sit with Rosie and over a drink we'd chat about anything and everything. Then when she reached the tipsy stage she'd tell me tales about her beloved Harry and have me in tears of laughter. Harry was, in Rosie's own words, a bit of a scally but a loveable one and she certainly loved him.

As so often with the drink flowing, private thoughts are revealed when in trusted company. I revealed to Rosie that my own marriage was over bar the shouting and although I knew it was inevitable it still hurt, but me and Jackie had agreed our son Lee's well-being was the priority. Respect would replace the sadness Rosie said, and she would be proved right. Rosie poured us both a single malt whiskey night cap. We toasted Harry and ourselves. We put our empty glasses down, hugged and bid each other goodnight. God I would miss Rosie.

One other good thing about working on the Erection gang for Henry Hargreaves was the money. The first week, on a Thursday, I got what I thought was my wage, to be told no, this was my expenses, my wage would be given to me tomorrow. Whoopee! I'd never been so well off. That first week I treated myself to a pair of Levis, a Ben Sherman shirt and best of all a pair of Ox Blood red loafers. Put together I looked the part, if I do say so myself.

Among Rosie's other guests was a girl called Liz Taylor. On being introduced to her I refrained from the obvious jibe simply because I thought she would have had a stomach full of it and I think she appreciated it. Well I know she did, she told me. Now I knew Liz enjoyed talking to me but as for chancing my arm romantically, I knew better. She was drop dead gorgeous. Maybe in the movies, but not in real life. All this changed one night when, after my tea, I asked Rosie where Liz was and she pulled me to one side and quietly informed me Liz's Nana had died and, as she had been raised by her from a young age, she was devastated. Rosie also asked me if I could see if I could tempt her out for a drink and a chat. "She's more your age and you're a good listener." Hesitantly I agreed.

I went to my room, smartened myself up then made my way to Liz's room. I knocked quietly three times, eventually the door slowly opened and I was staring at the saddest, most gorgeous face, the tear-stained eyes only adding to her natural beauty. "Liz" I stammered, I am really sorry about your Nana!" I was wondering if you would like to go for a drink or a bite to eat?" She looked at me and at that moment I just wanted to hold her. Of course I made no attempt to. Instead Liz put her hand on my shoulder, kissed me on my cheek and whispered "Thanks for the thought Eamon, with drink inside I would fall apart." I said I understood, but if she changed her mind I would be in my room. Then she closed the door.

I returned to my room and absentmindedly switched the radio on. The story being covered on the radio stopped me in my tracks, "Elvis is dead!" No it can't be! But they wouldn't joke about that would they. Eventually it sank in. It was true but how and why? I wasn't a big Elvis fan but I found myself upset and emotional. I decided to get undressed and along with the radio took to my bed. It felt so sad. The songs would play all night. It was approaching 12pm before my favourite track "I just can't help believing" began playing. I began filling up, by its end the tears were flowing. I was becoming drowsy, sleep was beckoning.

It was then I thought I heard the door creak but with the noise of the radio I wasn't sure. I was facing the wall in my dark room and frankly too dopey to check but even as close to sweet oblivion as I was, I sensed I wasn't alone. I turned, and with the aid of a sliver of moonlight that found its way into the room I was presented with the vision of Liz in her dressing gown stood over me looking very puzzled. The puzzled look changed to one of understanding. After shedding her dressing gown she slipped in beside me and whispered "just hold me".

As drowsy as I felt this would be a test for any red-blooded male. Lord help me now I thought as I slipped my arms around her lovely waist and held her close, with my head snuggled into Liz's neck, I don't know what perfume she was wearing but Lord it wasn't helping my cause to restrain myself. I now really wished I had worn a tighter pair of trolleys. To have this goddess almost naked so close was torture. I tried to think of something, anything, just not rude. I decided to mentally replay the match I had played the previous weekend. Brilliant! Only after scoring the winning goal it wasn't my team mates hugging me, no! It was Liz and she wouldn't let go. This was agony for my little member for Bury North. He gave his all to save the day and my dignity but above all Liz's feelings. Thankfully I must have dropped off after a while. I was woken by the softest of kisses. My eyes focused just in time to see Liz's gorgeous form making its way out of my room. Maybe it was all a dream. I thought maybe Elvis hadn't died. But it wasn't a dream although its memory would always seem so.

The next day being Friday gave me the impetus to get through the day albeit in a drowsy daze which when you're working on ladders 30 feet up is not good. Late that afternoon

Michael the chargehand informed me the following Monday I was to start work on the new Arrow Park hospital in Birkenhead. Michael asked me if everything was OK, that I was very quiet. I knew I'd probably not see Liz again.

That evening I said a very sad farewell to Rosie. On being asked she wrote the house phone number down which cheered me in as much as I might get to speak to Liz again. It wasn't to be. The following week I rang Rosie from my new digs in New Brighton and she told me Liz wouldn't be coming back but had a message Rosie was very curious about. "Liz says she will never forget you." This puzzling Rosie, I told her I'd comforted her when she needed just comfort. "Well done lad, and don't forget, keep in contact." I said I would but with the best intentions life gets in the way. Rosie and Liz both enter my mind on occasions, for completely different reasons.

There then followed a further 10 months which saw me relocate to Crosby and finally the Nat West building in London. The short time on the Nat West (the tallest building in London at the time) from the start of the six weeks I was there, on asking my chargehand each day what he wanted me to do, he'd reply "look pal, until I contact you, just take this red head gun" (for forcing screw attachments into concrete.) "Keep on the move and make it look like you're doing something." Alright, for a few days, not for more or less six weeks.

I was bored to death. On top of this I'd acquired digs at a place called the Oval Hotel near the cricket ground. My room, which I shared with two Geordie lads I struggled to understand, was situated at the very top of the stairs. No lift. In our room were three beds and for some reason they'd left me what looked like the better bed of the three, the others being supported by a combination of bricks and books. Mine was free standing with a wash basin I could literally reach up and touch while in bed. The reason for my roommates kindness became apparent after their first night on the town. In the early hours I was woken by what I thought was warm water spraying my face. I looked up to see one of the Geordie lads peeing in the sink drunkenly mumbling something about "loo downstairs." It was obvious the loo was four floors down so the sink was for the night and while staring out the window at the London skyline I knew the next day I would be out of London. And I can't believe it myself, phoning big Al again.

Al again didn't mince his words. "See you Monday". What a guy! I knew the first week I would come in for the expected stick: "My God back again", "Why do you bother leaving", "The homing pigeon returns". After that first week it felt like I had never been away. Strangely, I knew it wouldn't be too long before I would need to seek new pastures but for now I would keep my head down and hope something else would come up. Sadly Bry had left. He found employment in the building trade. Maybe just as well, Bry always had the devil on his shoulder, nothing nasty just high spirits.

Can't Say No

For some reason I was struggling to find contentment in my Saturday football, maybe it was our Pat's words, years before, that on the football Sabbath (Saturday) I must strive to play in the highest standard I could achieve. When I look back now I found myself playing in teams sometimes for years, as in the case of Prestwich Heys and Abbey Hey. Always with the thought at the back of my mind "what am I doing here?" If a manager of any team approached me saying he really wanted me I could never find it in me to refuse. This resulted in some crazy situations.

At one time in the '80s I was playing for Radcliffe Borough on a Saturday afternoon under Dave Morris, a smashing bloke who I had a lot of time for. Sunday morning I was turned out for the Roach, then Sunday afternoon giving my all for Ted Barry's The Grosvenor in the Blackley League. One of the lads, Dave Brown, who ran the Masons on Bury Road used to drop me at Whitefield bus station after the game, I'd then catch a bus that would drop me on Market Street near the corner with Wellington Road. There was a bench facing the bus stop, on that bench I would rest until I regained enough strength for the walk home. I ignored the common sense advice of family and friends. I couldn't face letting down these guys who believed in me and wanted me.

In the end something had to give. Towards the end of the season I'd twisted my knee playing for The Roach. It was really painful and I was really struggling to even walk. I phoned Ted to explain I wouldn't be able to turn out for him that afternoon. Ted said "you'll be OK for next week won't you, we're playing New Cross Celtic in the semi final of the cup. I told Ted I very much doubted it. He then told me he'd be picking me up the following Saturday afternoon and to make sure I was in. He prevented any protests by saying "I'll see you then" and promptly hung up. Mum and Pat were always suspicious of Ted. They must have got the gist of the conversation; they warned me not to let Ted railroad me into playing. My knee wouldn't be right for 3–4 weeks and that was that.

When Ted knocked on the door that following Saturday before I got there our Pat was already quizzing Ted about where he was taking me and telling him there's no way I'd be playing that Sunday. "Thanks Pat, I'm a big boy now. You ready Ted?" "So where are you taking him Ted?" Pat asked. I just looked at Pat. "To see Fred Street, Man City's physio, just to check him out." Our Pat's face was a picture. Suitably impressed, he kept his counsel. On the trip to Mr. Street's residence Ted was asking strange and cryptic questions like "if there was no more pain in your knee you'd be OK for playing? They have some fabulous treatments these days, don't they?" I just agreed with Ted, didn't know what else to say.

As we arrived at Mr. Street's place Ted said "Come on! Let's see what he can do for us." There was nobody else there. Mr. Street seemed a nice fella. He asked me to roll my trouser leg up on my injured leg. After asking me to point out the affected area, after doing so he drew a circle around it with a ballpoint pen. With his finger resting inside the circle he gently pressed as he asked me when I felt pain. Each time I replied another circle was drawn inside the original, until we ended up with a circle the size of a pin head. My system then took a jolt as Mr. Street approached with a rather large needle. I instinctively looked away and tensed up. God I hate needles. Almost instantly the pain had gone. I was astonished. When I entered the building I was walking very tentatively knowing any time shooting pain could take my breath away. And now, well I felt like a spring lamb. I don't know what was in that syringe but miracle cure wasn't too far from my lips along with the obvious questions born of an enquiring mind. Why would a pro player with a minor injury ever need to miss a match with this stuff around? And what exactly was this stuff?

It was Ted who told me, my miracle cure was cortisone. Thankfully this was my one and only encounter with cortisone as the downside to this miracle cure was simply that as you felt no pain you would be completely ignorant of damage you could be inflicting on yourself. I ended up playing in the semi final and scoring the only goal. Thankfully there would be no lasting problems.

During my time playing for Ted I would be introduced to a number of truly gifted and exceptional talents. There was Sonny Rice who must have been fifty when I played alongside him, apparently Sonny had been a Northern Irish international, watching him on the ball it wouldn't surprise anyone. Billy Bell could play football with the best of them. A powerhouse of a player, there was also a side to Billy that wasn't very pretty. Small incidents could provoke him and when he lost it, people who knew him didn't interfere, they knew better. I remember once being in the same Prestwich Heys team to face Mosley in a pre-season friendly. Billy's idea of warming up was to repeatedly nut the dressing room door.

Another player I remember well was Eddie Hearst. Eddie was a joy to play alongside, so gifted. I also have fond memories of Keith Barnes whose illustrious brother Peter would become a Man City legend. Keith I can honestly say was probably a better all round player than Peter, in my opinion. He also possessed a cutting wit. The guy loved a giggle. Ted being Ted sometimes asked me to play in a final, even though I hadn't played in any of the rounds, saying, because of injury and illness, he'd found himself short of players. Total rubbish of course. Ted thought I was better than what he had so he'd say anything. This happened once when we were playing Keith's team the Carters. Keith walked into our changing rooms, took one look at me and said "I don't believe it, it's "I'll see you in the final Eamon." Thanks Keith, it took me a good while to shake that name off. Playing in teams where I hardly knew anyone just to play in what our Pat would call a decent standard was beginning to lose its attraction.

Getting back to my roots to me at this time sounded just the ticket. It was time to play with my mates. It meant no money for playing but as I was to find, it would be the best decision in my long football life.

Another big decision

Summer of '82 would see me marry once more. Deb Coffey was a workmate. She was a Bolton lass and although I knew she was seeing someone I also knew she wasn't happy. I know it sounds cold but I was so glad when they finally split. I wasted no time in asking Deb if she'd like to go for a drink, with continued pestering she finally agreed. It was so good I knew that first date I had to be with this girl. Only about eight weeks had gone when I convinced Deb, against her better judgement, for us to rent a flat together. That place would be a couple of rooms in one of the big houses facing the Wagon and Horses on Walmersley Road. God it was grim. Deb would never allow any of her family to visit and I guess I knew why.

Funnily enough we had some good times in that flat, especially when a couple of our workmates moved in with their girlfriends. Craig Holden, his girlfriend Jess and Ste Bell and Debbie. These were two seriously funny guys and we'd be in and out of each other's flats. And when the weather was fine, me, Craig and Ste would grab a ball and go and have a kickabout in Clarence Park. There was a place where two trees were just the right distance apart to form the nets. We'd kick around to our hearts content while the girls had a natter. Deb was a bit wary of Craig but thought the world of Ste, she said he was the funniest guy she'd ever met. So it wasn't me then? We couldn't believe our luck when the council offered us a council house until we found out where, Kingfisher Drive, Dickybird Estate. Now don't get me wrong, I'm an ex Dickybirdian. But the estate had undergone a massive change since the days of my childhood blissfully happily spent there.

It had become, for want of a better word, rough. What the heck, beggars can't be choosers. So after work, me Deb and anyone else who'd give us a lift worked tirelessly to turn No. 45 Kingfisher Drive into a habitable abode. One night, returning to our Walmersley Road flat, walking in the darkness by St. Joseph's School, we were stopped by the police and searched. The bag I was carrying contained a claw hammer and a large screwdriver. Didn't look good, did it? But when your speaking the truth you tend to speak with more conviction. The policeman must have sensed this or maybe it was our dusty faces that convinced him, that night we were just glad to get home and rest our weary bodies. These would be very testing weeks. By the time we were married we were already living in our new home. Poor Deb still didn't feel she could ask her folks round. She told me her Mum and Dad would be upset if they saw where we were living. Sadly I understood her worries. The place where I spent such a happy childhood, where decent folk lived in a warm blanket of community mentality was now sadly hardly recognizable as that same place. But why, what happened? There was a definite change.

I didn't expect the same Dicky Bird of my youth, I just secretly hoped for some remnants and to be fair there were pockets of neighbourly goings on, but overall the heart had gone out of the place. It so saddened me. It couldn't help but affect your mood. My memories that were so fond seemed tainted. Some folk would say "get in the real world". To be honest the real world doesn't seem so appealing. We can only play our own little roles and hope the people living by the old values influence the others.

Me and Deb made the best of our time on Dicky Bird but I knew she was very unhappy, cut off from her folks in Bolton and her friends. We'd argue and fall out which left her even more desolate, quite often she would leave to spend some time with her folks. Who could blame her? One Sunday we were travelling back from Deb's Mum and Dads on the bus, just as we passed the bottom Bull at Breightmet we noticed a house for sale. We made the decision there and then to see if there was any way we could attempt to buy it. To cut a long story short the bank let us have a 100% mortgage on the asking price of £13,500. In no time at all we were moving again, this time into our own home, complete with a date over the door – 1861 – the same year the American Civil War broke out. The first few weeks after we'd moved in I was having recurring dreams about opening the curtains in the morning and the scene outside was the same as with the first occupants in 1861. In my dream the A58 outside the door was little more than a dirt track, blokes in tight strides and pointed shoes sat upon carts being pulled by huge, powerful horses. Stuck in the past again.

Dad's failing health came as a shock, not just to me, but to the whole family. The spectra of impending death was for other people, other families, not the Kavanaghs. We were all going to live forever. It just had to be so. Anything else was unthinkable. Sadly, as much as we tried to ignore it, Dad's health was steadily worsening. I was always in awe of my Dad. Thinking back he'd drink enough to sink a ship but come Monday morning, while I sat there in a semi-stupor, Dad would fasten his boots up with anything he could lay his hands on, string, strips of cotton, even copper wire. The donkey jacket would go on and he was out the door, rarely with a word to anyone. When he came home in the evening after a hard day's graft digging for England and Ireland he would shed the jacket and head for his favourite chair. Immediately one of my sisters would remove his boots while another sister would hand him a piping hot pint pot of strong tea. All this while Mum prepared a tea fit for a working man.

The idea of us all sat at a table was impractical, us younger ones ate our meal where we could, if nowhere else, then on the floor. After his tea Dad would take out his rolling tin and roll himself a cigarette. The cigarette would be smoked right down to the tips of his yellowed fingers. The remainder would then be returned to the tin. Only now I see the relevance of this habit. Dad would never see a doctor or for that matter a dentist. He was the old school Irishman, a rare breed. He was, up to this point, never ill, so the devil in a white coat wasn't a problem. Any problem teeth, thankfully rare were extracted with a clean pair of pliers preceded by a good shot of whiskey. The amount of blood was awful but mum's protests were ignored.

Maybe I've done Dad an injustice, painting him as bog Irish. He loved crosswords. His intelligence was obvious and like a lot of quiet men, when he spoke you listened. On rare occasions he'd reveal a great sense of humour. One evening I got changed into my tracksuit and runners, as I was heading out the door Dad asked me where I was headed. I told him the running track. "Which running track?" he asked. "The one around the corner Dad, on Wellington Road." "Sure you can walk it in ten minutes if you run." Right Dad.

I came home one night and the house was empty apart from Dad in the kitchen. He was in fits of laughter. He was over the sink, having washed some pots he had hold of a nearly empty plastic bottle of washing up liquid. "What's so funny Dad?" I asked him. Whereupon he squeezed said bottle which produced a rude sounding noise and dozens of little bubbles floating about him, which again set him off like a hyena, staring at me with tears of laughter rolling down his cheeks. Keep taking the tablets Dad.

But Dad wasn't laughing anymore. He didn't need a doctor to tell him something was badly wrong. He was eating well enough but the weight was falling off him. He'd only shortly been retired, life is so unfair. One night I was climbing the stairs at the top of which was the bathroom. As I neared the top Dad's painfully thin figure came into sight. He was having a shave in an attempt to keep up appearances. As I reached the top step Dad's pants fell round his ankles, it was heartbreaking, there was nothing to hold them up. I passed by, silently made for a bedroom, any bedroom, I needed time alone.

When Dad's time came all his family were round his bed. As he took his last breath we all were holding him, any part of him we could. Within seconds of his last breath there was a crack of thunder after which our Margaret said "Heavens opened up to let Dad in." It was too much for all of us, even the few who'd kept themselves together up to then just give in to the emotion. In a way it was a lovely way to go. As was the Irish custom, Dad was laid out in the living room in an open coffin and the whole family slept in the same room. Strange as it seems, I found those nights spent with Dad and the rest of the family where we'd talk 'till the early hours very comforting.

After Dad's funeral, attended by our Irish relations, it felt awful having to get back to normal. There was only John still living at home now, the rest of us all partnered off and having to get back to work, it just didn't seem right. Mum was lost, totally lost. In Mum's mind she wasn't needed by her kids anymore. In the best way possible she begrudged our independence and now the quiet man she adored had left her. It was no surprise when Mum's health began to fail. Cancer was diagnosed though Mum was ignorant of this knowledge. A family get together was arranged to decide whether to inform Mum or not. It was agreed, I think wrongly now, to put Mum wise to her condition. By telling her the truth, we achieved nothing but added fear to an already ailing lady. The saddest thing where Mum was concerned was when it came to the moment she needed her kids around her to hold her, not one of us was there. Now that's hard to bear.

John being the only one living at home at this time and as fickle fate would have it, he was up at the hospital all day. I received a call while at work at Antlers, it was Tom, our Mary's partner. "She's gone lad." "What do you mean?" "She's gone lad." I hung up the phone and started running, awful thoughts racing through my mind. "There's a van waiting at security" Alan shouted as I passed him. I jumped into the waiting van. It was old Bill from the Stores. He set off driving, it seemed to me like he was doing about eight miles per hour. I was too emotional for this, as Bill tried to make small talk I opened the van door, jumped out and started running like I've never run before. As I arrived at the house, tears streaming down my face, Tom was already at the door. "I'm sorry lad, she's upstairs." As I slowly entered Mum's room I could never be prepared for the sight that greeted me. Mum's passing had obviously not been an easy one. Eight kids and not one of us to hold and comfort her. Grafted all her life for this. By evening time we were all present. The circle was broken. No focal point for the family. Mum and Dad both gone. The woman who made everything all right with unconditional love was gone. What will become of us?

The days leading up to Mum's funeral were spent as with Dad. She would never be out of our sight until she had to. We were a completely broken family. We needed this time together, the nights spent relaying stories of Mum and Dad, we'd all be laughing then crying, then laughing. When the dreaded day of the funeral arrived we all put on our public faces. Us four sons proudly carrying Mum up to the altar at St. Bedes where Father Williams would put his all into giving Mum the eulogy she deserved. We all took our places at the graveside,. My nieces Shelagh and Melanie who mum had reared to produce these two lovely young ladies who stood before me now. As the coffin containing our lovely mum was slowly lowered I knew what was coming. At the exact moment the coffin passed below ground level an involuntary guttural whimper escaped from the two of them and it cut me like a knife. We all dissolved into our emotions. We made a solemn promise there and then, no matter where we all settled, we would get together regularly enough to please Mum and Dad.

A Dog Named Blue

Towards the end of '84 me and Deb moved into our new home in Bury Road, Breightmet. Finally she could invite friends and family round without being embarrassed. I never envisioned leaving Bury, in the end it came down to simple economics. Our house on Bury Road had been empty for a couple of years plus we were granted a 100% mortgage. So we left Dicky Bird for the relative luxury of our new Breightmet home. Our neighbours we found to be as good as you could wish for, soon after we moved in I was in the Peel on Rochdale Road after a game one Sunday when one of the lads Baz Cowgill entered the pub carrying a small bundle of fur which turned out to be an Alsatian cross six week old puppy. As soon as I set eyes on it I knew I'd be going home with it. On agreeing a price of £15 I talked our Michael into giving me a lift back to Bolton to show Deb our new addition to the family. I knew there'd be no problem there, one look into those puppy dog eyes and she'd be lost, just as I was.

Money was tight. Our joint pay from Antlers didn't allow many luxuries. But provided the puppy wasn't a fussy eater we'd get by just fine. After a discussion about his name we decided on 'Blue' from the film we loved 'Cool Hand Luke' with Paul Newman. I can honestly say that £15 was the best money I've ever spent, Blue blossomed into not just a gorgeous dog but funny, entertaining and loyal. During his

Our lovely dog Blue enjoying a dance with our Micheal!

time going through puppyhood Blue caused a fair bit of damage in the kitchen where he was kept. As me and Deb were working all day the poor dog was bored out of his head.

One day we returned home from work, looked through the kitchen window, Blue had torn the new lino we'd had laid into shreds and was racing around in circles. We knew then we had to improve his lot. We bought a good large kennel and he was exercised every day whether we were too tired or not. Blue's life improved and the damage stopped. To save money me and Deb would walk the distance in the morning to the next fare stage. As GMT increased their fare charges me and Deb found ourselves walking further and further, we drew the line when we reached the Three Arrows, now the Ainsworth Arms. When we reached Bury we then had the walk to Alfred Street to the Antler Mill to spend eight hours on a production line. Wasn't life grand?

You Will Listen!

Friday was a great day, a dinner time finish with our wages in our back pockets we happily clocked out for the weekend and set off for Rochdale Road, either to the Peel, the Roach or sometimes the Turf on Wash Lane. Everyone was in good spirits and if not the entertainers in the gang, Mick Green, Craig Holden and the brilliant Ste Bell would soon have you laughing. The bus journey back for me and Deb, well lets just say some of those memories I'd rather forget. Embarrassing or what, I like to think we just got caught in the atmosphere sometimes. God knows what the other passengers on the bus thought of us. In our defence working in a mind-numbing job on a production line eight hours a day five days a week, at the end of which you needed some kind of release, to help me through my own day.

I'd rigged a makeshift sound system using a Phillips tape recorder wired up to two one foot speakers, as you can imagine this set up could produce quite some noise. And what a noise, every Johnny Cash track I possessed. "I Walk The Line" "Cocaine Blues" "Orange Blossom Special" blasting out all day long. Brilliant for me, can't speak for my other workmates. I guess it says a lot for Johnny Cash that no-one ever complained. I broke the inevitable boredom by mixing in some fine Irish music.

There was a few of my workmates with Celtic blood in their veins and during some of the more powerful songs such as "Green Fields of France" and "Dublin in the Rare Auld Times" they would become quite emotional. I obviously felt the need to share my wonderful music with all and sundry. Strange thing is now when I'm on the bus, some young kid turns his MP3 player up high, playing some monotonous rap and I feel like strangling them. Shame on me.

From Production to Storage

Our working lives at Antlers was slowly but surely changing. The amount of imported cases from abroad was increasing monthly. To be honest these foreign cases were classier than anything we were producing, simply, because we as a production firm were stuck in the past. Our design of suitcase hadn't changed since the '60s. We just hadn't kept up. The writing was on the wall for us, for us and a whole lot of British industry. Different causes but the main cause being cheaper goods from abroad. The daily workload at Antlers was changing, more and more of us on production where moved to the warehouse to unpack and repack the huge influx from abroad. Also less industrial music flowed from any of the three remaining production floors each the size of a football pitch. The music of the combined sound of machinery mixed with human chatter was being replaced with the ghostly quiet of a handful of blokes patrolling what would become a row of huge warehouses. The modern interpretation of progress.

Once in a while I meet up with ex Antlerites. We joke about the Antler penitentiary remembering how we substituted the word Antlers for 'San Quentin' in the great Johnny Cash song of the same name. The whole workforce was devastated when Ste Bell soon after being released from Antlers was involved in a horrific car crash on the border with Bury and Heywood. Steven was declared dead at the scene. This was the fella who we, his former workmates considered the luckiest fella we knew. Raffles, football cards, draws, he was just incredibly lucky. Sadly when he most needed lady luck she was looking away.

The funeral was a trial, Steven was a great human being but religious in any way he was not. As the clergyman spoke of redemption, then proceeded to quote passages from the Bible it just felt wrong. Craig Holden nudged me, whispering in a choked voice, "go up there, say some words for Steven." I choked back my answer, "I can't." I looked around me. All of us, his friends, were just too upset to string more than a couple of comprehensible words together. So Steven was laid to rest without hearing our emotional outpourings, it mattered not. Anyone looking upon the devastated tear-stained faces of his family and friends gathered there would be left in no doubt as to the measure of the man.

Fishpool Utd. And Roach FC

The time had come to put everything else aside. Any lasting dreams of being spotted by some wandering talent scout were laid to rest, any lingering thoughts of playing in the highest standard possible were vanquished. Yes! It was time to play the beautiful game in the company of my family and mates, the bottom line being I'm going to enjoy it. I longed for the more relaxed come-day go-day approach. Don't get me wrong. Any match I'm involved with I will never give less than 100% and expect the same from my team mates. I'd hate to be sat in the bar after a match with energy to burn. That would really upset me. Standards etc. But after the final whistle no manager screaming abuse or team mates squaring up. Win or lose I want to leave the pub feeling good. You might think that's a lot to ask but it isn't because that's exactly what happened. Fishpool Utd. Was a team managed by a lovely fella called Pete Lockey. Pete's vision of football was simple. All the best things are. Get my players to a level of fitness where the demands involved in a hard fought football match were well within their capabilities. Also, and more importantly to play without fear. This is a far from trivial realisation.

The best example I can give you is remember a time when you scored a brilliant goal or if a defender made a world class tackle for about 10 minutes after you can do no wrong. Your confidence is sky high, a cavalier attitude kicks in and you're engulfed with a feeling of natural high. Now obviously you would be unable to sustain that

Fishpool FC – the early days. The young lad knelt in front of myself is a very young Matt Holland, who went to to Ipswich and Repulbic of Ireland fame! The other little fella is our manager Pete Lockey's son Matthew, who remains a credit to his old fella.

feeling for 90 minutes. But if you're playing without fear, chances are those occasions will occur more often. Pete was wise in his choice of players. He preferred lads who were already mates, he knew this would go a long way towards a good team spirit. This is exactly how me and my brother Michael got involved. When we were asked by Pete if we fancied coming down for pre season training on Redvales me and our kid saw no reason not to.

We arrived for the first session with a little apprehension as you'd expect, there was no need, among the lads warming up were some familiar faces, Graham 'Rossy' Rostron, Paul Ramlavl 'Rammy', Daz Mitton and the Nichols brothers, Stephen and Pete. Needless to say we enjoyed Pete's training and the after training drink in the Napier Pub on Bolton Street just as much as this gave us a chance to get to know the other lads and a good bunch they were. Our home matches were to be played at Peel College, a pitch that was a treat to play on. In our first season we didn't exactly set the world on fire. We were a bit hit and miss. As the season progressed so did we, by the end of the season we'd put a nice little run together and finished a respectable 3rd. Looking back I think we all knew we would achieve better things.

Team spirit was high, punters who walked into the Napier early on a Saturday evening assumed we won every week. After a few beers, won or lost, we'd have the crack. An added bonus was that several of the Fishpool players had joined with me and Michael playing for our Pat's team Roach FC on a Sunday which had really pleased our

A great night for Roach FC at the end of a very sucessful season, where our Pat and his sidekick Les Barloow were crowned Manager and Assistant Manager of the Year.

Pat. The Roach under Pat's guidance along with his new sidekick Les Barlow were building a real reputation as a force to be reckoned with in the Bury and District Sunday league. This would be the high point of our footballing days for me and Michael for the two of us agreed on how lucky we were to be playing for two teams so committed to enjoyment. Michael had recently finished his time with the Royal Navy and something strange had happened on his return. He took over the role of older brother, no words passed between us, just an unspoken agreement that would allow this communal morph to take place. Strangely enough, we were both very happy with the situation.

The times playing for Fishpool and the Roach were to be filled with ups and downs but was never boring. So many characters drawn together by the love of the game and the simple enjoyment of each other's company. A player will look back on his career and certain events in certain matches, for whatever reason, will be forever remembered. This proved so for myself when in May 1983, as a member then of Roach FC, we faced the Rose and Crown from Ramsbottom in the semi-final of the Yorkshire Bank trophy.

I loved semi-finals, they're so edgy and exciting, usually a lot more than finals, that have a reputation for falling flat. This one would be played at Lower Gigg, at that time the home of Highfield Utd., one of the best pitches in Bury. It turned out a hard fought encounter but I honestly believe we had the edge on the day. After falling behind twice our quality came through, our strike force that day was awesome by any standard. Colin Stephenson (Stevo), Mick Brooks, Ken Buggie and myself backed up by the likes of Carl Suthurst, Roy Grundy, Chris Brooks, Mick Williams (Willy), Mick Kavanagh and the special one himself, Paddy McSherry. Goals from Colin Stephenson and Mick Brooks meant the game after extra time was level which left us with a penalty shoot out. I would be the last to take one.

Luckily for me and Roach FC I wasn't needed, we went through to the final on Gigg Lane's hallowed turf, it turned out our opponents in the final would be a team many thought were arguably the best team in the league, The Derby Arms. They were managed by a smashing fella, Ian Parry, a guy who genuinely loved the game and his loyal adviser Tommy Allen. Between them they'd put together a formidable side indeed. Some of their names are legends in Bury's Amateur footballing circles. Eric Greenhalgh, Martin Farnworth, Paul Dickinson (PD) Peter Rhodes, Dougie Irvine. This was going to be one hell of a game. I was filled with a mixture of excitement and foreboding.

The Saturday before the final on the following Sunday morning I was struggling to relax. Our Pat had banned alcohol and requested early nights. I heeded his words, at 9pm I was in bed but sleep evaded me. In temper I shouted down to my wife Debbie who was watching a film on telly and demanded she join me in bed in order for me to get some sleep. She refused of course, I did what any grown up mature man would do in this situation, I got dressed, then stormed out the front door, slamming it behind me. "Now what am I going to do?" I thought. I decided to just walk and followed my legs.

I ended up, after a short bus ride, where else but Inspiration Point. I sat there in the darkness, moonlight reflected in the softly flowing water of the Roach. Calmness seeped over me and because I was now calm at last I could think straight. By the time I was making my way home to Breightmet an hour later, I was relaxed and ready for sleep. After mumbling an apology to Deb my mind floated away to sweet oblivion. The alarm was set for 7.30am It was switched off before a ring was heard. The bed clothes thrown back, I found my dressing gown and I was down to the kitchen preparing my usual match day breakfast of two soft boiled eggs and toast soldiers washed down with two strong mugs of tea. My kit bag I'd prepared the day before. After checking it half a dozen times, one more time wouldn't hurt. Size 7 moulded boots, shin pads, crepe bandage, tie ups, Buxton rub, bottle containing Wintergreen and Olive Oil, large rough bath towel, all present and correct. It was time to go. I kissed Deb at the door, she wished me good luck and she'd see me at the match where she was meeting her folk. I caught the bus on the short journey to Bury then the short walk to Gigg Lane I took my time, I was glad of the quiet before the storm.

In the time it took me from Bury centre to reach Gigg Lane I'd got myself mentally ready, I just prayed my body would follow suit. All the boys were there, no-one missing. This was the worse time for me at big games, my nerves always gave me trouble. Our Michael was as bad, we'd by jockeying for position to get to the loo to throw up. Soon as the game started I was focused and knew my job. As we were lining up for the kick-off I glanced round and caught sight of the comforting figure of Paddy Mac and I wondered how many of the other lads did the same. Paddy was one of those rare players who inspired the lads around him to rise above themselves. With Paddy behind you, you believed you could beat anyone.

Bury FC had played Wimbledon the day before, the match had been televised using a crude scaffolding contraption for the cameras. One of our friends Vinnie Crawshaw scaled the ladder to its platform in order to video our match. So we hoped we could make it worth his efforts. We got off to the best possible start when one of our midfielders Dave Fee headed us into the lead after 10 minutes. When Micky Brooks added a second with a sweet 25-yarder we were in seventh heaven, things got even better when Butch McManus got our third when he slid in a corner kick.

We went in at half time almost drunk on adrenaline. Pat and Les had the easiest of half time talks. (More of the same lads – keep focused.) Things couldn't get better and they didn't, almost from the restart Paul Dickinson went on one of his penetrating runs which left him one on one with our 'keeper Dave Jowett. As Dave came rushing out Paul pushed the ball past him and carried on to shoot the ball into the empty net. Before we knew what had hit us the score had been levelled 3–3 with 20 minutes left. One of our defenders, Chris Brooks, made a crude tackle on one of their lads about 20 yards out.

Our 'keeper Jowett shouted instructions on where to position the wall. The fella stood over the ball was one Mr. Martin Farnworth, well known to all us Roach lads, his deft left foot even better well known. As he slipped back to take the kick a feeling of foreboding descended on the entire Roach team. It was well founded. Mr. Farnworth curled a perfect free kick round the now redundant wall into the top corner of our net leaving Jowett no chance. It felt like the end of the world.

We were gutted and feeling very sorry for ourselves. Then it came. The master spoke. "Listen up, nothing changes, we all stick to our jobs, only now we work harder." Within five minutes we were level. I picked the ball up just inside their half, their defence had pushed up, Mick Brooks our centre forward was stood level with their two central defenders as I ran towards him at pace. I hit a strong pass directly at him and sprinted through the gap between defenders. Mick made no attempt to control the pass, merely side footed the ball behind the defence. No-one checked my run. This allowed me to take the ball right up to their 'keeper who never left his line. I feigned to pass the ball to his right as he went down with the outside of my right foot flicked the ball to his left. The reaction of our supporters told me what I already knew. My team mates jumping all over me was still reassuring. Four minutes left and a high ball was lofted into our penalty area. Indecision between Tony Lomax and Dave our 'keeper allowed a very surprised Pete Rhodes to force the ball over the line, some say with his hand. Only Pete knows for sure, the goal stood, we were beaten 5–4. But we had the consolation that we'd taken part in a match that would be spoken about decades later at the regular gatherings of members of that squad. The same squad that, before very long, would have their time in the limelight.

Pitches in Bury

Bury has always been a football town. Since I can remember and long before I can remember the most common topic of conversation with the men of the town was football. Sadly some of our local fields of dreams were more like nightmares. During my school days I was blessed by the fact I had the hallowed turf of St. Gabriel's playing field to hone my talents. After leaving school, myself and the rest of the Bury faithful were to ply our trade on pitches that at times were hard enough to merely walk across never mind attempting to control a ball while navigating ruts or swamp-like surfaces. This made the occasions when you were lucky enough to reach a final of cup or league as exciting for the fact you would be playing on a decent surface as playing in a final. I realise this is a personal view, there will be many who would disagree. And, to be fair, and I know it sounds like I'm contradicting myself, some of my best memories include blood and guts battles played out in six inches of energy-sapping mud. These were the games where the heart played a bigger part than the head.

While the brain was screaming for you to rest awhile, the heart screamed louder, you must make that tackle, you must run that 30 yards into space, battle for everything, give no quarter. I honestly believe because of the heavy pitches we were reared on, where brawn is a dominant factor, is one of the reasons the British skill factor was so far behind the continentals. Think of the young Brazilian lad learning his trade on pitches as hard as concrete. With the ball being so lively on the hard surface it's a natural progression that his control of the ball has to be higher than his British counterpart struggling through the mud. As a reasonably skillful winger I thrived on a decent surface.

There were some pitches in Bury that were conducive to good football, pitches that come to mind are, for example, the pitch that took its name from the huge factory situated at the end of Bridgehall Lane, Heap Bridge. The Transparent Paper Mill. I really enjoyed playing there. There was always a good atmosphere helped by club members, pints in hands vacating the Transparent club house on its raised perch about 20 feet up the embankment at the side of the pitch. Either standing or sitting they would form a large and vocal crowd. The Transparent Club house itself was very popular. Entertainment at the weekends was supplied by a mixture of well known and local talent. And, more importantly, it served a good pint. Sadly the Transparent pitch was claimed to make room for new houses a few years back.

Another decent pitch was lower Gigg, as the name suggests it was located at the bottom of Gigg Lane right next to Gigg Paper Mill. Originally used by our illustrious town team the mighty Shakers to train on. It would, in later years, be the home of one

Fishpool FC at our home ground, Peel College. The best days of my football life.

of Bury's finest ever amateur teams Highfield United, a name that brings instant respect among the Bury faithful and beyond. Walmersley's ground just off Woodhill Road at the side of the Winterburns factory was another ground used for finals. To be fair, some of the pitches I disliked playing on during the early part of the season were often in a decent state but as the weather worsened so did many of the pitches, bad drainage was a common problem, such pitches that come to mind because of this problem are St. Anne's pitch at Tottington - rogue horse hooves are said to be blamed for this pitch's problems. Bolton Road, home for many years of another of Bury's finest, Elton Fold FC. I remember one occasion racing up the right wing towards the Bolton Road end on attempting to put a cross in, my standing foot sank about six inches which left my kicking foot simulating a golf club digging the ball out of a bunker.

But by far the Daddy of them all was the Clarence Park pitch facing the Lido. How some of the games were allowed to go ahead was beyond me. Referees desperate for the money, who knows. I played in one match there and no fewer than seven players had their boots sucked off by the gripping mud. The pitches at Goshen playing fields were hit and miss, on many occasions the pitches could have stood a rolling. I don't know whether the groundsman was overworked or just couldn't be bothered. I could count on one hand the number of times I'd run out onto one of the Goshen's pitches and thought "This'll do for me."

The number of pitches well cared for were very few. At one time there were two pitches within the boundary of Bury & Radcliffe Athletic club on Market Street. During the '70s I watched a match between Moorside and Chesham. On show that evening were some great players such as Ray Pierce, Joe Heywood and a young lad who played a stormer that night, the lad's name was Pete Cooper who along with his brother Jimmy would mature into a couple of Bury's finest. Their father would be at the helm of arguably Bury's most famous amateur team Chesham Fold. Chesham achieved great success over the years in the Bury amateur league as well as the Bolton Combination.

The Arrival of a Legend

The setting was innocuous enough, Peel College playing fields on a fine September afternoon. Two local sides, Seedfield FC v Fishpool FC. The game was about 20 minutes old, my brother Michael had hit a cross field ball from his left back position over to my right wing area. Hit at pace I just failed to keep the ball in play. The ball was picked up by a fella who'd been stood with our Manager Pete Lockey. As the guy turned to hand the ball to me I was looking into the face of a man who, as a highly excitable 13 year old, on watching him strike a perfect 25 yard drive that left the back of the visitors that day Bournemouth's net bulging, being his fourth goal of the game to take the score to 4–0 it was too much for my teenage mind, in one smooth movement I'd hoisted myself on to the hallowed turf of the Gigg Lane pitch, raced to my hero's side and hugged him with all my might. "Magic George, that was magic. That was magic." "Ta Son." Then with his right hand he ruffled my hair. George Jones ruffled my hair. Don't think I washed it till Christmas.

Well George was staring right back at me now. "Alright George?" He replied with a courteous "Alright son?" but he didn't seem to recognise me. God George it's only been about 19 years, remember I'm the fella who's hair you ruffled at Gigg Lane Bury V Bournemouth 67–68 season. "When you're ready son." The referee's shout fetched me back to the present. For the rest of the first half I was conscious of George watching so I did my best to show him what a great player I'd grown into. As so often happens when you try too hard, you achieve very little so I only succeeded in showing George what a gormless footballer I could be.

Half time came and George was still chatting to Pete. As us players trudged off the pitch Pete passed the bucket containing half oranges. Lovely. As we sucked on our oranges, Pete secured our attention by introducing George to the rest of my team mates. I had been staring at him since I left the pitch along with a gormless smile. Pete began "Good news lads. George here has kindly agreed to take training and maybe even turning out for us." Me and our Michael's faces were a picture. George Jones' name was always spoken with reverence in the Kavanagh household. Our Pat insisted on it. We shuffled closer together and let out incoherent noises at one another. Let's just say the thought of training and even playing alongside a legend left me and our kid babbling like imbeciles.

The second half for me was played out in a robotic state and judging by the run-around their winger was giving our Mick it seemed he was the same. At the final whistle I'd no idea whether we'd won, drawn or lost, the sight of our lads congratulating each other should have given me a clue. In the Napier that afternoon all the talk was about George joining us in our efforts towards success in the 85–86 season in the Bury amateur league. Up to this point we could be likened to Bury FC themselves, infuriatingly inconsistent. On our day we'd beat anyone; thing was we never had enough of our days.

Pete had put a lot of work into assembling a decent side, we just needed some fine tuning; and who was the man for the job? Who better than Sir George Jones? His first night as trainer was patronised by every member of Fishpool FC. Now I had never been a fan of training. Over the years I'd trained under many managers, some better than others, some honestly thought they hadn't done a good job unless they had you throwing up after each grueling ball-less pre-season session. But this was something else, this was done, dare I say it, yes it was fun.

George's style of training rarely didn't include a ball at your feet. We'd start off with some stretching exercises followed by some shuttle sprints. George would then cordon off an area of the field, after separating us into two teams with the aid of yellow bibs. Six consecutive passes was a goal. This was brilliant, it forced the team in position to run into space and the other team to close them down as fast as possible. Knackering but so productive. George introduced us Fishpool lads to a varied array of ball skill exercises one in particular comes to mind, you began with the ball at your feet then progressing backwards, moving the ball along with the soles of alternative feet, giving the impression of an Irish jig.

As me and our Michael awaited our turn George quipped "you two should be good at this." Our kid was before me, as he set off with the ball a few of the lads began chortling "oh diddly eye, diddly do, diddly I di dee". Michael collapsed in bits to the floor and I went the same way. Normal service resumed when two teams were established for our final kickabout. Using cones for nets, one at each end, as there was no need for a 'keeper. Andy Naylor, our outstanding man between the sticks received personal practice courtesy of Mr. Lockey. George's influence was instant and that following Saturday when he walked into the changing room at Peel college and began getting changed I thought I'd died and gone to heaven. My God, I'll be playing alongside a guy who'd achieved what I had always dreamed about, played pro football.

The thing was he just seemed a regular guy, no edge to him, I'm sure I even saw him going to the loo. Before the match started Pete and George called us together and imparted some words of wisdom that I scarcely heard, I just wanted the game started so I could learn all I could from George. Pendle FC who were our opponents that day seemed to me to possess no sense of occasion, were they not aware of who was lining up to face them? Well they soon would be. Some folk, eh?

The game proved a tough one, Pendle were no mugs. As I said George's impact seemed immediate, players up to this time who for one reason or another were playing below par were now galvanized into an efficient unit. When George spoke we listened, here was an ex England youth, Blackburn Rovers and Shakers player. George had lived the dream and now he was willing to get down and dirty with the common folk. I can't tell you how good that felt. 10 minutes remaining with the score at 1–1, one of the Nicholls brothers bagged our equalizer. Gary Wilson, a cracking little player, threaded his way down the left flank and as he reached the bye line he hit a lovely high cross that sailed over the whole crowd of players in the Pendle area, arriving at speed to the lurking Mr. Jones at chest level. In an almost poetic movement he'd taken the ball on his chest and as the ball hit the turf and was about to rise he hit such a sweet half volley it would have seemed an affront to common decency for anyone to attempt to hamper the ball on its only rightful destination. Some things when they happen just seem right and this was one of them. Obviously things didn't always go to plan. But overall we all knew we were involved in something really positive that would be beneficial to all concerned.

Most people during the course of their life will pass through a period of time that can only be described as special, you're almost afraid of saying it out loud in case the spell is broken. This would be our time. As that first season with George and Pete at the helm wore on, training at Peel College would remain well attended. George had hit on a radical idea of actually training with the ball at your feet 90% of the time. Radical indeed in our green and pleasant land. Even when the snow came and we had no access to changing rooms, cars were parked up along Wellington Road where lads would change their footwear for the conditions they faced.

George was an ever present, this was no 'Good Time Charlie' – here was a guy who'd see things through. One evening our final kickabout was played out in a snowstorm, hardly able to see more than a few feet in front of you, it says a lot that when the shout of 'Next goal winner' went up it was contested by both sides as if it were a semi final. Our little club was enjoying a spell in its history where each and everyone of us club members were thoroughly enjoying our football and because we were enjoying our football we were playing our best ever football. Fishpool FC already held a reputation for always enjoying their after match get together, won or lost. Only now the football was that bit more enjoyable.

The season would see us make headway in both the Kenyon Cup and the Parks Cup culminating in us reaching both finals to be played in the same week beginning with the final of the Kenyon Cup on Wednesday, 30th April. In both finals our opponents on both occasions would be one of Bury's most celebrated amateur clubs Chesham Fold, a name that demanded respect. When I'd last come up against this classy outfit a couple of decades before in a pre-season friendly, their line up that day was like a who's who of Bury's finest.

These are some of their players I remember from that day; Mick Forrest, brother of John, ex Bury FC and a great 'keeper in his own right, Alan Whitehead, Alan went on to play for Bury, then, if I remember, joined Altringham. Bob Barras. Bob came from a footballing background, his old fella played for England no less. The maestro himself Wolfy, what more can I say about Wolfy, Graham Booth, Mr. Reliable and a smashing fella to boot (pardon the pun.) Brian Green, the Bobby Moore of Bury's amateur scene. Ian McCool, a truly great player, uncompromising. Johnny Barrat; John looked anything but a footballer - darts player maybe but another who epitomised the phrase "looks can be deceiving" this was the fella. As a defender second to none and on his regular forages up front if given the chance he could hit a ball as hard as anyone which very often found the back of the net. Hutch would never class himself as an athlete, probably stoop for the term mixer, a good old fashioned centre forward who'd generate you 20-30 goals a season. Derek Butterworth, probably the classiest defender I knew. He also bucked trends. At school we were taught never to play the ball across our own box. Derek took great delight in flouting tradition with his own array of nutmegs and stylish sidesteps. Paul Lomax (Lou) to me epitomised everything positive in the game. Tough as old boots and a fine athlete who always gave his all. Paul could hurt you but if he did it would be fairly; a fellow Dickybirdian I'd always admired, not just as a footballer but as a loyal friend too. Pete and Jimmy Cooper (The Skinners). Pete the younger caused a big stir among the amateur establishment, Everyone agreed he was a bit special. He could score goals for fun, you couldn't take your eyes off him. His brother Jimmy was no slouch either. They'd no need to court favour with the manager who happened to be their old fella Charlie.

At one stage Chesham Fold outgrew their limited opposition in Bury and so sought new pastures in the form of the Bolton Combination. They then outgrew the Bolton Combination and sought sterner tests in the top local league The Manchester League. After working their way up they were denied top division status because their ground at Hoyles playing fields wasn't up to standard. I often think how far Chesham Fold could have gone. It seems a crying shame. We'll never know. One thing we do know this was arguably the finest amateur team assembled in Bury's history.

Back to the task in hand. We're at the Saturday before our meeting with Cheshom Fold in the Kenyon Cup final the following Wednesday. Our opponents were, that afternoon, Hargreaves FC. Their player-manager Ian Chesters being a genuine hard working lad, asked the same qualities from his team. This would be the perfect preparation for the final. George and Pete advised us players to give this game our all. They said we wouldn't be seeing another ball till Wednesday, the reasoning being with three full days rest we'd be chomping at the bit. So we heeded their wise words and give our all.

Poor Hargreaves must have wondered what was going on. We were like men possessed. How the game finished with us only scoring four goals I'll never know but that's how it finished, 0–4 with Dave Fee netting a brace, the highlight being the sight of Rossy netting his annual goal, running up to the ref and giving him a huge hug. Rossy's fading eyesight was always going to be a problem. In the Napier later the lads seemed a little subdued. I put it down to their exertions on the field that day. Only Mark Strong (Pongo) and Rossy were being themselves. Loud and daft, only joking lads!

Whether thoughts of the final on the hallowed turf were creeping into the lads' minds who knows. It was at this time Pete chose to inform us we'd be without our talisman George for the final on Wednesday. I for one was gutted and I knew the rest of the lads would be as well. The circle would be broken just when we needed to be at our strongest. Why? Why can't he play? Pete explained he would be away on holiday with his wife; he'd tried to change it but couldn't. The only good news being he'd be back by Friday for the Saturday final. Well that's something. We left the Napier and went our own ways, after shouts of "See you Wednesday bright and bushy tailed." Despite the feigned humour there was an unmistakable feeling of unease, I know from outside it would seem overreacting over the loss of one player and usually I'd agree but on very rare occasions a player with a huge presence and outstanding qualities comes along and right or wrong you come to rely on them. Amazingly we had George with Fishpool on Saturday. We also had Paddy Mac on Sunday. How lucky were we, lucky until for whatever reason they were missing, then what? Going into battle without our leader, the faint hearted would break rank, we'd end up getting routed. I know, over-reacting again. I told our Michael to make sure to get a good night's sleep on Tuesday night and just hoped I'd do the same. Does everyone get like this or just me and our kid?

Debbie has reminded me many times since what a pain I was leading up to those big games and, as for the night before, she took no chances and went back to her folks for the night. She'd remind me how unbearable I'd been in the past at these times. Demanding a brew, demanding she'd join me in bed at 9pm and because I couldn't get off, play with my hair till she was sure I was asleep. "I know, don't remind me," I explained these sort of games were few and far between. Deb just stared at me. I could never look her in the eye when she did this. Guilt I suppose.

Colour Blind

Wednesday came around. My work day at Antlers was spent in a robotic absent-minded state, being continually interrupted from my day dreaming of scoring a great goal at Gigg or better, still having a Matthews-like final on my sacred right wing. People would talk about my performance for years to come. I wondered if these thoughts were travelling through the other lads' heads. It would be no use asking them, these are not the things you admit to. I was sharply fetched back to the present by Agnes, our chargehand, demanding to know why 15 blue suitcases travelling down the conveyor belt had red handles on them. I just stared at Agnes. "Just get them off Eamon and get your mind on the bloody job you're getting paid for." I got to work on the affected cases among shouts and jeers. "Jethro you wanna borrow my glasses?" Greenie and Mick Gent were laughing so much they couldn't get their breath, thanks for small mercies.

When clocking off time came I told Deb I'd see her and her folks at the ground. The kick-off was at 6.30pm so no time to travel to our home in Bolton. Our Michael was to pick me up outside Antlers then we would travel to his home just off Cotswold Crescent, Walshaw. As soon as we entered the house his wife Anne set about preparing our pre-match meal of two soft boiled eggs and toast soldiers. After which, we downed the last dregs from our tea cups we were on our way. The three of us set off with Anne driving, obviously conscious of mine and Michael's pre-match nerves she kept relaying reassuring comments like "just go out there and give it your all, no-one can ask anymore." Wise words but sadly very ineffective. As Gigg Lane came into view I felt a distinct tightening in my chest and my breathing was becoming irregular. One look at our kid told me he was experiencing the same ailments. All I could muster was to say "we'll do alright when the game starts our kid." Luckily there wasn't long to go to kick-off. After retrieving our bags from the boot we made our way apprehensively to the changing rooms deep inside the North Stand.

As we entered the spacious changing room, Pete our manager ushered us in, asking where we'd been and telling us to hurry up and get changed. There was plenty of chatter among the lads as they put the final touches to their immaculate new kit, bought specially for this final. I looked around in the vain hope of seeing the one face I already knew wouldn't be there. Stupid or what? After securing my last tie up I made my way to the loo, this would be for my customary big match throwing up session. Confronted by a locked door, I knocked loudly, saying "get a move on Michael else I'll be throwing up out here." Our kid emerged ashen faced, as sickly as I felt. I couldn't help laughing at the situation. "Do you think we'll ever change our kid?" "Nah." After emptying the best part of my previous meal, then pulling the chain, I joined the rest of the lads lining up alongside our illustrious opponents Chesham Fold.

Like gladiators about to fight to the death we warily eyed one another secretly hoping to find weaknesses in their armour; heavy colds, headaches, a touch of leprosy maybe. No chance, they all looked like thoroughbred racehorses. Forget the psychology, lets just give our all and to hell with the rest. As we walked out onto the hallowed turf, God-it felt good. The shouts from the gathered faithful, short on numbers but very vocal, had me feeling a little giddy. During the kickabout I looked up into the stands and waved at all the family members. As the referee's whistle sounded to bring the two captains together I looked around at my team mates and by the expressions on their faces I was in no doubt what this meant to them and to our little club. A win against the mighty Chesham Fold would put us on the football map. Chesham had had their glory days just maybe it was our time.

The whistle blew once more and battle began. As expected both teams were pumped up, tackles flying in with no quarter given. There were scenes at both ends with nerves or indecision presenting both teams with half chances. With both defences dominating and direct shots at goal a rarity, it was no surprise to go in at half time with the score 0–0. Peter our manager was beaming as we took our seats in the changing room. "Well lads I'll tell you now, this is your night. The score will be one nil and I'll even name our scorer." We were dropped on. Has he lost it or what. "Go on then, who's the scorer," one of the lads asked. "Daz Mitton." While Daz looked very excited at the prospect, doubt and worry about Pete's mental state prevailed. Pete must have sensed this and proceeded to take £50 from his pocket, placed said money on the rub down table, looked around and said "Any takers?" Well needless to say there weren't any takers. Pete was just so damn sure.

A little bewildered we made our way out for the second half. Ten minutes into the second half you could see it and sense it. All through our team and to a man the confidence was high, the touch assured and as our confidence grew Chesham's shrank. For the next 20 minutes we lay siege to their goalmouth. Joe Cassidy went close with Pete Nicholl even closer hitting the bar with a close range header.

Then at last came the breakthrough. Paul Taylor played a lovely through ball that caught their defence square, young Paul Ramlavl (Rammy) sprinted down the left flank with all their defence running back and all us forwards racing in the hope of meeting Rammy's inevitable cross. When it came it was a wicked cross, whipped in at pace evading the glut of players attempting to meet it. The ball floated to the edge of the penalty box where our No. 10 Ste Nicholl met the ball perfectly, executing a beautiful volley that fairly rocketed into the top corner of the Chesham goal. Their 'keeper never moved a muscle. Is there a better feeling in the world than moments like that, it's tangible and so emotional. We weren't content to hang on for the final whistle. The best form of defence is attack and attack we did and that's what we were doing when the final whistle went. Pete had been so clever; he knew some of us were being hampered by nerves. He knew confidence was essential to reach your full potential. So he played a confidence trick if you would. And I must admit his gamble paid off handsomely. We'll let him off as to getting the scorer wrong. In the Waterloo that night many pints were sank in celebration. And a well earned toast to Peter and our absent hero George.

On parting company later that night we reminded each other that there was to be no drinking Friday. Why? Because its back to Gigg on Saturday. It was no use telling Rossy about the drinks ban. Rossy loved his Friday nights and come hell or high water he'd be out. To be fair, drinking never affected Rossy's game, he was always bobbins. Seriously he was one of the lucky ones, he could have a skinful and still be fresh as a daisy for the match. Rossy was the team's whipping boy, the stick he took was merciless. A blind imbecile with a face only a mother could love. Sounds terrible doesn't it but there was no malice. Anyone with an ounce of sense could see beyond the taunts. We loved Rossy. There was never a dull moment with Rossy about. Fact is I've seen Rossy up Bury at the weekend with some of the loveliest girls in town on his arm. This backs up the theory 'girls just wanna have fun'.

The days leading up to Saturday seemed reluctant to end, as it was to be an evening kick-off. I promised Deb I'd stay calm and nerves wouldn't set in till Saturday afternoon, the same time Deb would be joining her folks at Tonge Moor, Bolton. Later that day the whole family would set off together destined for Bury's famous old ground in the hope of seeing a repeat of the previous Wednesday's brilliant result. So there I was five hours before I'd need to set off, the only question – how to spend the time? Something relaxing. Music would be good but what music, country or Irish? No, not today. Today I needed to really relax. Classical fit the bill and as I only possessed one classic tape of Strauss that would have to do. Tape set to play, got comfy in my easy chair and tried to think of anything but football. After deciding to pull the coffee table over to use as a footrest I picked up the book lying on the table. Don't know what it was that gained my interest, the attractive hard back cover or the title itself 'Wuthering Heights' by Emily Bronte. I hadn't read a book since 'The Wind in the Willows' at Junior School.

I felt fidgety so thought what the hell and began a dark, sad, angry, wonderful journey through Emily's book. I'd seen the film, this was nothing like the film. I'd hear folk say the film can never match the book, I now knew what they meant. I was so engrossed as I finished the final page I was overcome with emotion, almost bereft. I was shocked a book could have such an effect on me. It was nothing short of a revelation. My God! What time is it? 5.30! We were kicking off in an hour. I threw two slices of bread in the toaster before they popped up I was ready to go, two minutes of impersonating a Key Stone Cop and I was at the bus stop facing the house waiting for and praying the 471 bus wouldn't be late. It wasn't, even so it was 5.55pm when I arrived in Bury.

No time to dally, straight in a taxi. "Where to Eamon?" "Hi Mo". Mo was a friend who'd served his time at the Antler penitentiary. "Gigg Lane cocker! Fast as ya can Mo." On the short journey to Gigg Lane me and Mo caught up as best we could. We parted with me asking him to give my best to his brother Jim who was also an escapee. Time for my first sprint of the night. I arrived in the changing rooms about a minute before I set off. "Where the bloody hell have you been?" "Sorry lads." Within four minutes flat I was changed and covered in olive oil and Wintergreen. "Borrow your rub Eamon?" It was my hero George. I'd forgot George was back off holiday. We weren't sure whether he'd be back or not. What a shot in the arm, George heading the attack.

As I watched a naked George rubbing my Buxton rub all over his body an involuntary shout of "George" escaped from me. "What? What's the matter Eamon?" "You shouldn't. Oh never mind. Come on lets get out there." No time now to worry about Buxton rubs reaction on the more sensitive parts of the body when combined with hot water. Time now to focus on the job in hand, made easier tonight with the inclusion of the architect of our previous triumph. As we walked out once more onto the worn surface of Bury's famous old ground, this time to contest the Parks Cup, our Michael was right behind George and I was right behind Michael, his face furnished with a gormless smile and I knew exactly how he was feeling. We were walking out on to our Wembley alongside our childhood hero. The incredible thing was George looked just as proud. All I could think at this time was how many times had he done this and been greeted by a deafening roar.

The crowd tonight was larger than the previous Wednesday. But a deafening he won't be getting. In the warm up after waving at the folks in the North stand that tonight housed a decent crowd, I glanced over to the Chesham Fold team going through their own warming up exercises. I felt no fear. Sure there was still quality there, a couple of the younger lads were my team mates on Sundays with Roach FC. John Davidson (Big Bird) was one funny lad who would mature into an excellent player and a funnier man, and Mick Brooks, a member of the original Roach FC that started life on our makeshift pitch under the one Arch. There were even several lads from the glory days. George Dunn, Mick Lord, Dave Smith and the still fearsome Paul Lomax, already praised within these pages.

But something was missing, what, I don't know. I'd always thought of Chesham in the same light as the Liverpool side of the seventies. If you came away from either without a good hiding it was a fantastic result. Well those days were behind them. Tonight was about the cherry on the cake. The perfect finish to an almost perfect season.

As the referee's whistle sounded, confident Fishpool FC set off efficiently and with no small amount of flair to their task. To give credit to Chesham they were in no mood to roll over. They would do all they could to gain victory. Two defeats in one week by Fishpool United was unthinkable. Their efforts were rewarded, Chesham's Mick Brookes ran on to a through pass from what seemed to us an offside position. Dave Wilson the linesman and father of Gary, our left midfielder, kept his flag down, no favouritism there then. Brooksy pushed the ball a couple of yards and hit what we used to call a 'daisy cutter'. The ball hit powerfully from 25 yards or so, never left its slide rule path about six inches above the ground till it rocketed into the back of our net. To beat our 'keeper Andy Naylor from that distance wasn't easy.   Half time came but there was no panic. We trudged off to the changing room leaving behind supporters who were enjoying themselves despite the scoreline. There was no need for heated words in the dressing room. There never was at Fishpool. Anger and screaming orders or threats weren't conducive to healthy fearless expression. Pete was the first to speak. "It was a great goal from Brooky lads, offside or not. This second half, chances will come our way. Let's make sure we take them." George was unusually quiet. Also looking distinctly uncomfortable, pulling the neck of his shirt outward as if letting out imaginary steam. His flushed face prompting our kid to ask was he OK. George didn't hear him. As he was about to go over to George I caught him by the arm and whispered "leave it". A little puzzled Michael finished his cup of tea and joined in with planning our second half victory. As we were walking out for the second half our Michael said to me "there's magic in the air tonight our kid." I knew exactly what he meant.

On rare occasions, even facing what appear to be incredible odds, a warm reassuring entity seems to enter your body and settles mind and body, furnishing it with the complete belief that anything is possible. This can take place usually at crucial times in a person's life. It's not restricted to the soccer pitch. But tonight I thank God for it. For the short time it burns within, life is grand.

The second half was only 10 minutes old when we were treated to a vintage George Jones goal. After a scramble in the Chesham goalmouth the ball was only half cleared, falling at the grateful right foot of the man himself. The trigger was pulled and through a glut of players the ball found its way into the net. We were all over George. He even got a kiss from Daz Mitton. Happy days.

The defence again dominated. Every promising attack was to be thwarted by two determined defences. It became obvious to break the deadlock it would take something very special or a terrible error. Well thankfully we got the former. Joe Cassidy picked up a loose ball in his own half. On reaching the halfway line he let fly an outrageous effort that was still rising when it hit the back of the Chesham net and sent our handful of supporters wild with delight. I've witnessed some wonderful goals scored at Gigg Lane but none better than this, Mr. Cassidy had produced a moment of pure magic. The cherry was on the cake, our job now was to make sure it stayed there.

We battled and fought and contested every single ball for the remaining 15 minutes. The sound of the referee Ken Rudge blowing his whistle was bliss. After congratulating each other then shaking the hands of the defeated Chesham Fold team I made my way to shake the hands of the officials which included one Gary Wilcox, no mean player himself and brother of my old mate Mark. There then followed a short ceremony where Fishpool United were presented with the handsome Parks Cup. Holding the cup aloft we were rewarded with the welcome applause from our small but enthusiastic supporters. I was first in the showers and first out, I knew what was coming. George having been under the shower for a couple of minutes came rushing out like a scalded cat. "Eamon! What the bloody hell is that rub you gave me! I'm on fire!" "I'm sorry George, I tried to tell you but by the time I'd noticed, it was too late. It's Buxton rub, to be treated with respect, mighty powerful."

I sat in the Waterloo that night soaking up the atmosphere and occasionally having a laugh at George's expense due to him resembling a strangled turkey. Well if it ain't 'George I'm so embarrassed Jones' followed by the inevitable Indian calls. I remember everything till last orders. From that time on I remember nothing. I woke up on Sunday not feeling right well really. Deb fetched me a cup of tea up with some toast, then she said "I've ironed your stuff for work tomorrow." Back to reality.

Sadly I was a member of the Chesham squad that during the 1991 season turned up for a league match with 8 players following weeks of struggling to field a squad. It proved too much for our joint managers of Paul Lomax and Jimmy Cooper. It was the saddest occasion of my football life, when Paul and Jimmy said "that is it boys, that's it for Chesham Fold". I couldn't believe such a great club as Chesham Fold could finish up like this. No great send off, no fanfare, nothing. Very very sad.

Home Improvements

The rest of the year would be mainly spent renovating as best we could a house that had been forsaken for over two years and it showed. Money was tight so we were restricted to cosmetic improvements only. Even so, after painting the rendered front and rear we were well pleased with the result. As the year wore on small improvements here and there produced a pleasant enough abode, a fitting reward for our toils. After a chat about finance it was decided I needed to look for a better paid job. A little restricted inasmuch as I left St. Gabriel's at the tender age of 15 with nothing to show in the way of qualifications and no trade skills. The question was what talents, if any, would entice a prospective employer?

Bury was a great little town for the folk who sought gainful employment. The problem was I needed to make the most of my modest talents. Hard working and when appreciated, very hard working, courteous and I enjoyed the company of like minded folk. After a fruitless journey on my bike round my newly adopted town and Debs home town of Bolton, I arrived home a little downhearted. Debs attempts to cheer me up were appreciated but ineffective. Neither of us knew then but the following day would be the day when a decision would be made that would change the course of, and greatly lighten the financial net we were in.

I can honestly say I'm not materialistic, I was content with our Spartan way of life. Not being a fan of the throwaway society I hated waste and what comes with it, its simply unsustainable and an embarrassment to decent minded folk. To save enough for our annual holiday to Torquay wasn't easy, after paying our deposit, in order to raise the money we'd need, as a favour, I'd ask my foreman Bob to put me down for any overtime going. A couple of times I ended up cleaning the boiler. This required me to don a white canvas suit with oversize Wellington boots, I was so thankful I'd be working inside the boiler even though I'd be working on my own.

On top of what little overtime I put in I'd ask around for anyone needing odd jobs doing. Sometimes it was close but we always managed it. The one year we didn't was awful. For one reason or another that year our cash was eaten up. It seemed a long, long year. You have to have the carrot dangling in front of you, its what keeps you going and makes it worthwhile. The next day being Saturday, the football Sabbath, Deb would go see her folks and I'd usually do very little before my afternoon exertions on the football field. We'd just finished our breakfast when there was a knock at the door. As it was unexpected we just sat there staring at one another like a pair of fugitives on the run. On the second knock I answered the door. It was the postman with a package he needed a signature for. On signing for the package I handed the pen back to the postie, as he took it he said "I hope you don't mind me asking but did you ever play football for Prestwich Heys?" I think I over excitedly answered "Yes! Yes I did!"

He informed me his name was Paul and reminded me of a game I played against Hyde Utd. in a cup match under floodlights and we won 1–3. I remembered the game well, I felt magic in the air that night. I loved playing under floodlights and I loved playing at Hyde Utd. It was a lovely little ground and the majority of their supporters genuine football fans. That night I felt so good I was itching for the whistle to start the game. By half time we were two up and I'd supplied the crosses for both. The second half saw Utd. Pull one back then ten minutes from time I scored an absolute peach. I was almost moved to tears by the sight of their supporters clapping me. I don't know who their full back was that night but I almost felt sorry for him. This was the time postman Paul chose to tell me it was him. "You're joking!" "No, it was me," he said. "I've been having therapy ever since." We both cracked up laughing.

After a while Paul asked me what I was doing for a living since it was obvious I hadn't hit the big time. After informing him of my disenchantment with the job he said "why not be a postie?" Paul told me he loved the job, good exercise, socially rewarding and the best of all decent money with plenty of overtime on offer. It was something I'd never considered, why I don't know. It would suit me down to the ground. This would be the last time I'd see Paul. Months before he'd put in for a transfer back to his hometown of Manchester and this was to be his last day working in Bolton. After shaking hands we wished each other the best. His parting words were to stay with me. "Don't forget what I said, be a postie, you'll love it." Deb had been listening to the conversation. She agreed it would be great if I could get on. "Do you not know anyone who's a postie who could put a word in for you?" After pondering a while it came. Paul Lomax, the Iron Man. The rock what Chesham Fold rested on. Deb said what have you got to lose, go for it.

Paul Lomax, as you've probably guessed is someone I admire but I had only a vague idea where he lived. I knew it was somewhere in the Walmersley area. I also knew the almost perfect Mr. Lomax had one weakness. He loved the horses. No he really loved the horses, not just betting on them, he genuinely loved the horses themselves. As I knew of only one bookies on Walmersley Road, I reckoned paying it a visit would prove fruitful. I would see Paul when Fishpool played Chesham again but that wouldn't be for a good while. No. I was too excited at the prospect of becoming a postie. God hope I'm not setting myself up for a great fall. It's too late for anything today. Got to get my mind back on football, Tottington Utd at Town Meadow, kick-off at 2pm. I don't believe it, the clock on the wall said 1.30pm with what seemed like a sneer. I flew out of the house kit bag in hand. Thankfully the bus arrived just right, even so it was nearing kick-off time when the bus pulled into Totty terminus, Peter our manager was standing on the corner of Market Street outside the Robin Hood of which an upstairs room was serving as a changing facility. As I approached him Pete was very animated, arms going like a windmill. "Where the bloody! Get up there and get changed, they've already kicked off and we've a bare eleven with you, so for God's sake hurry up. I mumbled an apology as I flew up the stairs, Pete made his way to the pitch a hundred yards down the road. It would have taken Pete about three and a half minutes to get to the pitch and soon after the cavalry would arrive. Who am I kidding, I knew a few of the lads would rip me for missing kick-off and I don't blame them, second time already this season, not good enough, our Pat would say, not keen enough.   As I trotted down the alley off Kirklees Street I headed for the touchline gesturing to the ref that I was here. Almost immediately everyone around burst out laughing. For a second I panicked and thought "what's going on?" Then I noticed our lads were attired differently from me. What a plonker. "I'll nip back Pete" "Oh no you won't, there's a shirt here, shove it on and then get on." A smiling ref signalled for me to come on. The game finished 2–2. You can imagine the stick I took in the bar afterwards. Even their manager Paul Leach quipped "Eamon, if you wanna be a Totty player just tell me, no need to go impersonating one. Ha ha."

The following Sunday I rose early to turn out for my Sunday team formerly known as Roach FC but due to another disagreement with the landlord we would now be known as Peel FC. Our after match drinks from now on would be drawn by the more than able Dennis Dagnall and his trusty helpers. The Peel up Rochdale Road was a magnet for the local lads and girls. Dennis ran a tight ship. He wasn't the most social of fellas but you knew where you were with him.

To Blackburn and a Giggle

For now I needed to get my thoughts on the match to come. It was the quarter final of the Lancashire Trophy, we were to play Gregson Lane Fold at Queens Park in Blackburn. Because of the importance of the match our Pat had hired a 40 seater coach to allow our small band of dedicated supporters to add their vocal encouragement to our efforts on the field. We arrived at their neat and tidy ground with time enough to get the feel of the pitch, as with every big match me and our Michael with nerves getting the better of us were jockeying for position for the loo. The only two nervous wrecks in the team happen to be from the same family, says something. We were in good form and our star men would be on show, Trevor Lewis, Col Stevy, Paddy Mac, Mick Brooks. Four of the finest. And playing at their best gave us a chance against anyone. The match turned out a nervy encounter with neither side settling into any rhythm. No goals and few chances. The referee's final whistle signalled the end of a stunted performance from both sides. We hoped for better when the second leg would be played at our pitch three weeks later.

As the saying goes 'behind every cloud……..' well the journey home after a few pints at their local proved to be our silver lining. It started with one of the lads asking me to "tell us a joke Eamon." Me, fancying myself as a bit of a comic, thought it was a grand idea if for no other reason than to cheer up the unusually subdued teammates and supporters. I felt a bit of pressure here as the whole coach was quietly waiting to be transformed from subdued to hilarity by the power of laughter. Trev Lewis, no mean comic himself, said he'd back me joke for joke. Sounds good but this first joke better be a good one. "Come on Eamon, your audience awaits you."

Here goes. "Paddy on a first date, trying to impress his new lady said "I've got a brother at university." "Really, that's wonderful" the girl said. "Yes, he's in a glass jar in the biology department." The lads were falling about. Buoyed up by their appreciation I was just about to unleash another cracker when Trev chirped in "my turn!". Trev's joke went as follows: "Bloke talking to other bloke about their pets. First bloke says "my dog plays chess. Second bloke says "that's fantastic, so clever." First bloke says "not really, most times I beat him."

From that moment till the time we arrived outside The Peel hotel in Bury, me and Trev played joke tennis to the sheer delight of our trapped audience some of which were in a helpless state from laughing their way through the whole journey. It was an event that no one involved will ever forget. These days everyone has stacks of jokes on their mobiles, everyone's a comedian. The likes of me and Trev are now redundant.

New Suit

Within the next few days I was to make the trip to the betting shop on Walmersley Road and it was to prove fruitful. Although Paul wasn't to be seen, his brother Alan was, Alan directed me to a big fine house where he knew his brother would be as he'd just been talking to him. I knocked on the impressive door, the entrance to this fine Victorian four-storey end terrace. (I'm not obsessed with everything Victorian. I would prefer it if some were Tudor or Elizabethan.

As you'd expect I received the traditional Lancashire welcome, a good firm handshake followed by a cup of tea being placed in the same hand. After a couple of hours of yesterday's wine and the main reason for my visit to which Paul promised to put a word in for me with Royal Mail. I thanked him for his time and promised to take it easy on him when Fishpool played Chesham in two weeks time. Paul's wry smile told me he knew I fully intended to stay well clear of this powerhouse of a man. I would seek an easier passage. The following week I received an official letter from Royal Mail informing me I was to attend an interview the following Monday at their Crompton Street office. I won't even attempt to describe my feelings on receiving this letter, if I'd won the pools I couldn't have felt more excited.

The following Monday I turned up at the office on Crompton Street. Decked out in a new suit I tried to convince Deb the price of the suit would be an investment. No pressure then, convinced or not the suit was bought and here I was sat in front of four ominous looking fellas who would decide my future. Secretly hoping the suit would carry me through the interview in spite of me not responding appropriately to certain questions. I was thankful when one of the fella's said "well Eamon we'll be in touch." I shook hands with all gathered, probably a little too enthusiastically and I was then shown to a small room and was shocked when a couple of sheets of paper were placed in front of me. I was instructed to fill them in and they would be collected in a short while. Oh God please don't forsake me now. They were test papers. While the questions didn't seem too hard, my nerves were jangling and as a result of this my mind would go blank. When the man came back after around half an hour I nervously handed him my papers, it was out of my hands now, fate would decide my future. Confidence deserted me as I made my way home. I couldn't even contemplate failure, it would be just too much.

Mentally I'd already left my job at Antlers. If my application proved unsuccessful I honestly didn't know what I'd do. Despair beckoned. A couple of weeks later a letter dropped through our letter box. I couldn't open it, I couldn't even touch it. I looked at Deb then left the room. She knew what this meant to me. She would do what she knew

Me doing a convincing immitation of a postie.

I was unable to do. I sat in the kitchen head in my hands, breathing very erratically and dreading the words that would break my heart. Debs scream of "Yes! Yes! Was balm to the pent up fear inside me. We both ended up dancing round the living room till we both collapsed in joyful exhaustion. The letter informed me my application was successful and I was to begin my life as a postman on the 19th January 1987, a date indelibly written in my psyche.

The Royal Journey

The appointed day arrived and though it was one of the coldest days I can remember, dressed in my ill fitting grey Royal Mail suit and proper peaked hat sporting a gold Royal Mail emblem I don't think I could have been happier. I would spend many many happy years with Royal Mail, over those years covering every corner of the fair town of Bury. My journey with Royal Mail as a postie would be punctuated with some real comical events. You'll be able to judge for yourself later. During my first week's work I would be accompanied by an experienced postie called Billy Fish who's real name was Billy Maddox. Maddox – Haddocks – I know, very loose connection. The round I was to take over was called 'Stormer Hill;' the start of which was a small firm called Melco located behind the bus terminus at Tottington and ended at Shepherd Street in Greenmount. I would then cross a farmer's field, on reaching the style at the end of this field I would come out on to Longsight Road directly facing was the bus stop. I would wait hopefully not too long for my journey back to town where after my lunchbreak I would set out with a handful of letters to complete my second delivery. My first day under Billy's supervision was very enlightening!

One of the houses on the round was a lovely old rambling house dating back to the late 1700s complete, as I found later, with a resident friendly ghost who, when the mood took it, would tinkle the ivories on the beautiful grand piano that had pride of place in the exquisitely decorated guest room. In times to come on a couple of occasions when I was caught short, on being allowed in by the lady who cleaned there, through thankful eyes I drank in the splendour of the place. This lovely house named 'Vineyard Close' was owned by a professional couple named Foxtrot. Often after delivering to our local entrepreneur Ron Woods enormous but characterless abode at the top of Station Road Greenmount I would take the short cut through his garden gate and walk about 30 yards to be greeted by the vision of the ancient but wonderful 'Vineyard Close'.

As I've already admitted, I love history, especially local history and luckily for me my round, Stormer Hill' was crammed with history. Back to my first day when after closing the gate behind us me and Billy made our way up to the door of the wonderful 'Vineyard Close'. As I went to post the two pieces of mail I was startled by bloodcurdling barks of what sounded like a huge dog approaching fast. "Billy" What do we do Billy!" I glanced round and just caught Billy's right hand disappear over the garden wall to join the rest of his fearless body. My fears proved true when I was confronted by the biggest snarling Alsatian I've ever seen. My first action was to place my delivery pouch between me and said dog. There was no way I was attempting to move, the stand off was broken by Mr. and Mrs. Foxtrot answering the door to see what was causing the row. I was very thankful for their arrival at the door. Their joint shouts of "Rebel, here!" immediately calmed the dog down. Mr. and Mrs. Foxtrot apologised profusely and insisted I come in for a stiffener. I was just about to decline when I thought 'why not'? My heroic workmate Billy will have to wait a short while while I have my stiffener which turned out to be a lovely drop of single malt which I thoroughly enjoyed.

Me and the Foxtrots exchanged niceties; this would be my one and only meeting with them. I made my way out through the gate to find my awkward looking colleague who commenced to explain to me his dog phobia that was born from a terrible experience he'd had as a child. Billy finished his explanation by saying "well no harm done, you handled the situation very well." My reply was I'm just glad I wasn't in the trenches with you during the war."

Our next destination was Tower Farm, a working farm. Facing Tower Farm was a row of cottages known as Tower Terrace. As Billy waited by the farm I made my way along delivering the cottages' mail. On returning I was astounded to find Billy playing with the Farm's border collie. The face on Billy! "Oh! I have known him since he was a pup". "Right Billy, that is a bitch you're petting". During our working life together me and Billy would have many heated discussions concerning our work but overall I liked the fella.

Another place of historical interest on my meandering postal round was Brookhouse Farm owned at that time by the Ellis family. Originally the farm was owned by the Woods family. Success in farming brought the Woods family moderate wealth. Henry Woods was born in 1603. This strong minded young fella would mature into a strong minded big fella who would have a big influence on many local folk. During Cromwell's short reign as 'land protector' Henry's disillusionment with the purists' ideals led him to join a movement started by George Fox eventually to become the Quakers.

What I liked about the Quakers was while they had their own beliefs they were very open to other views even to the point of inviting them, as long as those views weren't an affront to their Christian lifestyle. A breath of fresh air when compared to the rigid doctrines of the religions of the day. Trouble for Henry came in the form of Charles the Second once on the throne the Quakers were told to conform to the Church of England. Henry's reward for ignoring the royal command was to have his cattle taken from him. Standing firm in his convictions, the brave Henry would spend many years in jail. Jail in those days was far removed from the privileged establishments of today. At the grand old age of 80 this incredible fella set off on a voyage with his son John. Their destination – the land of the free: America. They set off from Liverpool and later that year landed in America where they founded the town of Woodbury, New Jersey. The good folk of Woodbury and Bury are today actively involved in making the long journey both ways in order that their young folks can enrich their lives by sharing in each others. See what you started Henry.

Round the back of Brookhouse Farm is Brookhouse Mill, now occupied by Cormar Carpets. There's little left of the original mill that is actually named in Cromwell's Doomsday Book and just up the road lies Quakers Cottage and Quakersfield, a row of back to back cottages. Strangely, I was to deliver the mail to the back doors, not the front. About this time I was becoming preoccupied with date stones, if I came across any old looking house or building I became almost obsessed with knowing its age. Crazy.

During my first few weeks on Stormer Hill I'd still be on my second round at 3pm, my second delivery taken up with snoop like jaunts round any half interesting building, and on this round there were plenty of them. I'm unsure where my preoccupation with the past stems from. I've often thought about it, maybe I hankered after the security of former dependability. Its hardly peculiar to myself, when we meet up with friends we haven't seen for a while, not all the time, but a good part of it is taken up with 'yesterday's wine' when the world seemed more stable. Having said that I remember the Cuban missile Crisis in 1962 when I was an impressionable 8 year old crying with fear in the company of my older sister Sheila. The terror we both felt as we watched the two super powers go toe-to-toe in a face off that could end with nuclear oblivion. This moment in time had a big impact on my young self, that has without doubt influenced my character. That aside I found myself doing a job I loved and will continue to enjoy for many years to come. My working day began on entering the old post office delivery centre on Crompton Street, the hours preparing the mail for our rounds were spent in the company of jovial workmates who were only too eager to help any colleague who was struggling for whatever reason. I knew that after the war Bury Post Office along with many others around the country was largely populated by ex army lads. The feeling of camaraderie that existed then could still be felt now.

Two giant characters at Bury office were Clifford Leach and Harry Greenhalgh You'd have to travel many miles to find two finer men. At times it seemed to me they were put on the earth to make life that bit sweeter for all around them. Similar in character in as much as their come day go day, let tomorrow look after itself attitude was very infectious. They were literally on a high with life itself. Clifford would fetch me a brew each morning then proceed to give me a lift before he even started his own round. One day while delivering to Albion Mill at the bottom of Bolton Road as I was about to enter the building I was surprised by Harry coming up behind me asking me to take a parcel to the top floor with the mail. "Course I will Harry" I said. Leaving my post bag in the foyer I made my way to the top floor where Ashworth Slippers had their offices. On returning to my bag shortly after I was shocked to find all my parcels missing. Then the penny dropped. What a guy. Some folk restore your faith in mankind. What a lucky fella I was - from a high pressure production line, to a job I loved so much getting out of my bed in a morning resembled a Cornflake's advert.

The winters could be challenging but come the spring, bag over my shoulder, no-one looking over me, the sun on my back, strolling through our green and pleasant land. Well Tottington anyway. I'd always enjoyed the company of my fellow man and my new job certainly lent itself to that. No day was quite the same and because of the distance I was covering was keeping me fit. Near the end of my round each day I would be treated to sight of the home. I, Eamon Kavanagh after winning the pools would purchase. 'Vineyard Close'. My dream home. Imagine my horror when years later returning for one more longing look at the magnificent building I was confronted by some modern characterless monstrosity in the space previously occupied by the proud Vineyard Close. To say I was upset wasn't enough. How could this be? I stood there staring, hoping my senses had deceived me. But no, there was no mistake. With my mind in a whirl I called round to one of my old customers on nearby Station Road. She informed me Mr. Ron Woods who occupied the end house on Station Road had Vineyard Close demolished to make room for his new home. But how would he have gained permission? It had to be a listed building. She just shook her head repeating "I don't know." I left so saddened, I never found out the full story. I just hope Mr. Ron Woods had a damn good reason for his actions. I often wonder what would have happened to Vineyard Close's resident ghost. Hopefully Mr. Woods owns a piano, otherwise who knows what he'll be up to to pass the time.

Crompton Street to Wellington Street

Royal Mail's decision to leave their home in Crompton Street after 100 years and relocate to the then vacated MFI building on Wellington Street in 1991 was for many of us a sad time. We knew it had to come; the old office was struggling to accommodate an ever expanding workforce. This being a direct result of Bury, like many other towns up and down the country, was itself expanding. It seemed every bit of vacant land was a target for housing projects, industrial units, whatever. The old office, as small as it was, had plenty of character. Each work frame was tight up against one another so chatting to your workmates wasn't a problem. Our rest room had in its centre a full sized old snooker table which was always occupied with would-be Steve Davis's. Because of its central location, trips to the shops or bank were made easy. The new premises on Wellington Street were certainly spacious but along with their old building something else was lost.

Ramsbottom office, established in the mid 1800s was to close its home on Bridge Street and join us in Bury. It must have been harder for the Rammy lads than us simply because their office was tiny which led to a family atmosphere which sadly the new office did little to nourish. As time passed changes would come that chipped away at the very essence of what it was to be a postie. I realise this would have been happening in all industries but to me this was one of our final links to a bygone time. And it made me sad. I know no one can halt the march of progress but without a doubt we'd be losing something.

Bury was expanding rapidly, on the occasions I did overtime I'd find myself in areas I was familiar with but in the short while I'd been a stranger, had acquired a new housing project. It seemed wherever I found myself, down Gigg Lane, on Woodhill, Birks Drive, Brandlesholme or down Manchester Road I'd have mail for places I'd never set my eyes on before. Being on the post certainly gives you an insight into our town's continued expansion. Good, bad, necessary, who knows? Each year saw an increase in the weight on our backs. Trolleys were available but the truth was trolleys would put up to an hour on the time to complete your round. This reason alone meant very few took up the offer.

The younger posties seemed to me to be in continued competition to break the world record of shortest time to finish their round. Us older posties just passed wry smiles between ourselves watching our younger colleagues racing around. The man who epitomised the relaxed but efficient attitude of a good postie was my old mate Kenny

Buckle. (Benny Cuckle). Don't ask! I can't remember ever seeing Kenny flustered; even his Scots flavoured accent emitted calmness.

Being well known as the slowest postman in the office, my lack of speed, no problem in the early days, was now and then creating situations which left me in a stressed state. Kenny found these events puzzling. "Why are you stressed? It's not a rat race." I knew he was right but I had to get all the bags ready for the driver so he could drop them off at allocated points on my round. This meant on heavy days more often than not I ended up in a stressed state; once out on the street I was OK, it was in the office I was struggling. The other lads and girls seemed to breeze through their time in the office. Julie, a girl I first became acquainted with as a youngster, living with her mum and nephew at their home in Proctor Street, now years later was working beside me. Julie was a very attractive, athletic lass of Jamaican descent. We became firm friends and would spend many hours just chewing the cud or playing her favourite pastime, tennis. With Julie there was no taking it easy because she was a girl. And if she thought you were she wouldn't think twice about giving you a winger. To say she is opinionated is putting it lightly. We had some real rows in which we both would stand our ground and me being a fella would do the natural fella thing and sulk. Never for too long though when you were working as closely as we were, it was hard work if you weren't talking.

The first task of the day involved sorting boxes of mail into separate boxes which each represented someone's round. This part of the day I enjoyed as we sat side by side sorting the mail we had the chance to have a chat and a giggle. Our own little group contained four of us, Tommy the Tank, a lovely fella who had a Mensa IQ and whose brain I picked on a regular basis. Me, Julie and John McLoughlin, a lad I never saw eye to eye with but none the less admired his single mindedness. John decided one day he wanted to be the best in his sport of body building and he succeeded to a certain extent, reaching a point where he became Mr. Great Britain in his weight category.

We all got along just fine. Every now and then me and John would get into a full blown argument over one subject or another. I knew for my safety when I should have quit but for some reason I'd carry on and end up on the floor. Alas no lesson would be learned, there was no way a Kavanagh would back down merely because someone was bigger and stronger. I realise this may sound the height of stupidity but that's the way it is, and to be honest I wouldn't have it any other way. I think I should say at this point our arguments were few and far between. Harmony reigned over our little group in the main.

New Round, New Challenge

One grey January morning in 1989 I was called into the manager's office. I was then informed I'd lost my round to a senior man and was now allocated the round named 'Hinds'. I was familiar with Hinds, it ran from the Bridge Trading Estate at Bury Bridge as far as Epworth Grange nursing home, just before Bolton Road playing fields, the then home of Elton Fold FC and in width took in Elton Sailing club and on to Woosnab Farm. The round was named after the old Hinds mill that at this time provided a home for the fleece merchants 'Strong and Fisher', most of the working in producing a luxurious clean fleece was done in what can only be described as a huge wind tunnel. A friend of mine who worked at the mill, situated in the Daisy Field area of the town, between the River Irwell and the Bury Bolton Canal, said he hated the job. In winter it was freezing and to get the smell of rotting flesh from his body half hour showers were common.

It was a good half mile from Florence Nightingale Hospital to Woosnab Farm, my first stop would be the sailing club. Here, if Old Tom the steward was around we'd always have a little chat. A straight talking, no nonsense chap, I found Tom refreshing and always enjoyed our chats. Just to the side of the sailing club were two large Accrington brick semis. No. 1 High Bank was the home of the local milk man Cyril who also had a small sideline producing moulded figurines for the garden. On some days you'd pass Cyril's and with all the figurines in regular formation they'd look for all the world like a terracotta army. Next door at No. 2 was the one and only Manuel Maleski, the darling of the St. Gabriel's female pupils and, because of his escapades on the football field, the hero of us lads. Sadly his football career waned a few years after leaving school, he gave up the beautiful game and sought solace as an inventor, rarely venturing further than Preston's paper shop facing the Wellington Pub on Bolton Road to collect his paper. Manuel seemed happy to live a very secluded existence with his mum and dad at their remote home in peaceful surroundings, taking daily walks around the surrounding countryside. Woosnab Farm was the home of a lovely lady named Sheila Todd and her husband and folks who, years after I left the round, every Christmas, would send me a box of chocolates, delivered to the sorting office.

Daisyfield Court had as one of its residents none other than Texan singing star of the sixties P.J. Proby, alias Dave Marcus Smith. As a kid one of the first singles I bought was P.J.'s 'Hold Me' a brilliant record. I played it so often you could hear the B side. He was also famous for splitting his pants on a regular basis, being engaged to Dean Martin's daughter and getting married at Bury Registry office. At this time P.J. was fighting his problem with the demon drink. It seemed to me most of the time he handled his problem very well. Always polite and chatty, P.J., when venturing out liked to be adorned with his trademark Stetson. Well over six foot he cut an impressive figure. His situation saddened me, how could a fella reach the peak of fame and fortune as P.J. certainly had to now find himself living a Spartan existence on his own in a flat in Daisyfield Court. The only visitor I ever saw at the flat was a small mousy lady who came by now and then to clean for him. I assumed she was a fan from way back. Although I was told PJ was often seen enjoying a drink in one of the many watering holes on Bolton Road. P.J. took over the flat from another of Bury's characters, Haz Brindle of Fuddy Duddy fame. Anyone from Elton was familiar with Fuddy Duddy. During the '80s they were the resident group at the Eagle and Child on Bolton Road. And very good they were, with Haz lead singer, Paddy Kirwan on drums, Brian Gabriel on guitar and I can't remember Paul the other guitarist's surname. For the regulars of the Eagle I suppose things got a bit stale but for someone like myself who rarely drank down Bolton Road they were a treat. Sadly Haz passed away recently. One less of the great characters that colour the town of Bury.

Incredibly one day while delivering to Daisyfield Court I had a special delivery letter for one 'Frank Ifield'. No, couldn't be, I thought, and I wouldn't blame you for doubting my sincerity but I assure you I kid you not. On knocking on the door it was answered by none other than the unmistakable man himself. I can't tell you how much I was tempted to break into a chorus of "I remember you...oo....oo....!" Thankfully I restrained myself. Turns out Mr. Ifield was visiting friends, staying with them a while before returning to Australia. I loved my job.

From 1990 for a couple of years part of the round I was on, Stephen Street, took in Grange Road. No. 67 Grange Road at this time was the home of the Neville family. I hardly need tell you of the success enjoyed by and earned by Gill and Neville's two sons, Gary and Phil. And let's not forget their sister Tracy who went on to represent England in her chosen sport of netball. What a fruitful union it was when their mum and dad got together. Three kids, all internationals. At the time I was delivering to them their two lads were just breaking into the first team and, as a result, there was a definite increase in mail and recorded packages, to the point where I came to an agreement with the boys to save disturbing them early mornings I'd sign for the packets myself and leave them in the gas box beside their front door. This arrangement suited all concerned.

One day while delivering to the Neville home my eye was drawn to what looked like a large pendulum clock protruding from their dustbin. On closer inspection I found it to be exactly that. It was a handsome specimen and not a mark on it. My mind was made up. The fact that the bin men were at the top of the street merely seemed to convince me I was on a mission of mercy. I knocked on their door, seeing this as common courtesy before relieving someone of the contents of their dustbin and, receiving no answer, I tried next door, to no avail. I then carried my ill gotten gains over the road to a friend's house named Paul who agreed to mind said clock 'till I'd finished my round, so I could collect it with my empty bag. One hour later I returned to Paul's to collect the clock. Paul informed me he'd replaced the old battery with a new one and it was working perfectly. "I suppose now they're famous, rather than change a battery they just replace the whole thing," he quipped.

The bus trip home was a little daunting. The clock standing around two and a half feet tall, a good third of it was protruding from my pouch. You can imagine the comments I received from some of the passengers travelling on the packed 471. "Time to clock on then?" "Have you got the time pal?" "Even if it doesn't work It'll be right twice a day." At times like this it's so maddening when you can't think of a witty response. So quietly I completed the journey home.

On rising to get off, to my dismay, the clock chimed the hour, the cue for some wise guy, as a parting shot to exclaim "that's a striking clock mate" which was rewarded by the bus in uproar of laughter and my extreme embarrassment. That clock has been adorning my kitchen wall ever since and as with any ornament that has held its place for many years you pay little attention to it. All that changed when one Sunday a while ago I was listening to Manchester radio, I think it was Alan Besick, anyway his guest that day was Tracy Neville. They asked if anyone was interested in ringing in to talk to Tracy about her career. I think they were taken aback a little when I rang telling them the story of the clock. Somewhat puzzled, expecting a sporting question, but being a good sport, Tracy laughed at my confession about raiding her dustbin years before. She remembered the clock well and informed me it ended up in the dustbin as a result of its erratic chiming, sometimes choosing early mornings to go on loud chiming sprees. Why they didn't merely switch the chime mechanism off completely as I have done is a mystery.

The lads at work kept asking me about organising a football team to enter the Bury Amateur league. The lads seemed really enthusiastic about the idea. In the end I agreed. Although still playing Saturday football, my workmates' enthusiasm was infectious. I always found it so hard faced with folks sincere in their appeals, even if I had my own reservations. George Jones, my hero, had left to seek new challenges which made the decision a little easier. The following season saw, after an absence of many years, a team of Royal Mail players represented in the Bury amateur league.

After pre-season training and a couple of friendlies it was obvious to me we were no Barcelona. We had a couple of handy lads, Paul Kent, Paul Sharman and Bernard

Creswell come to mind. But depending on the standard in the league at that time, I had reservations mostly about the lads continuing enthusiasm if we were getting whipped every Saturday. That first season was a real trial. We'd been allocated Town Meadow off Kirkless Street, Tottington as our home ground. We would get changed in the outhouse at the back of The Dungeon pub. We were all set. Predictably we had a couple of unremarkable seasons in the Bury amateur league. Having said that there was one game I could never forget. Towards the end of our second season we had a fixture against Radcliffe outfit, Groundwork Landscapes. They were an intimidating outfit who employed dubious tactics, why I never understood, as they could be a good footballing side.

Anyway, we took the field at their home ground up Outwood Road. From the kick-off they tore into us, completely overpowered we collapsed. We took a mauling. The final whistle came as a blessing. Us Royal Mail players trudged off the field with our tails between our legs on the wrong end of a 13–0 thrashing. Yes 13–0. As a team that night we all sought solace in alcohol, and plenty of it. By the end of the night the verdict was they were lucky. All their goals were breakaways. Yeh Right! The thing was the following Saturday we were to play them again in the quarter-final of the Parks Cup.

When we took the field the following Saturday at Redvales on Manchester Road let's say confident we weren't. Incredibly with 20 minutes to go it was 1–1. Then it

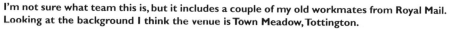

I'm not sure what team this is, but it includes a couple of my old workmates from Royal Mail. Looking at the background I think the venue is Town Meadow, Tottington.

happened. I was brought down just outside their box. Our midfielder Paul Kent placed the ball for the free kick. Two steps backwards, then two strides forward he struck the ball so sweetly it seemed almost inevitable it would arrive unobstructed in the top corner of the net. Paul ended up buried under the ecstatic bodies of his team mates. Because of what went on the week before it made this extra special. The remaining minutes were torture. All of us nervous wrecks, the beautiful game was forsaken in favour of the big boot anywhere. A corner for them in the last minute fetched our nerves to snapping point. The ball was floated over, their centre forward met it perfectly. His header rattled our bar, came out and was booted up field with all he had left by one of our defenders. Before they could collect the ball again the wonderful final whistle went. Reluctant hands were shaken and us Royal Mail players spent the afternoon high as kites talking absolute rubbish, but feeling mighty grand.

Not This Season Lads!

My round would take me to revisit a place I'll always have fond memories of and unknown to me at that time I would once again turn out representing our newly reformed Royal Mail team. That place was the Old Doctors just off Royds Street.

Even now as I looked towards the old changing rooms memories of Dawson, McCool, Taylor, Bell, Morrissey and Tommy Allen cracking some gag as we left the changing room heading for the pitch. Why is it everything seems sweeter looking back? Totty Utd were the new caretakers and along with their well respected manager Paul Leach it would be in good hands. The following season I'd made the radical decision not to take part, the reason being a worthy one, although friends and even family were, lets say, unsure. Deb was tired of spending every weekend on her own and not being a football fan, watching my teams wasn't an option. If I'm honest I'd known for a while Deb wasn't happy. Like many blokes, I'd just chose to ignore it. Well Deb had decided I wasn't going to ignore it, not by anything she said, simply how she was in herself. And if I knew Deb she'd just do one. One thing I knew, I didn't want that.

So my football was put on hold in order to save my marriage. Most weekends I'd see my son Lee from my previous marriage. The usual routine was that I'd collect Lee on a Sunday morning early, he'd then watch his old fella do his impression of Stanley Matthews, wait outside the changing rooms for said old fella to emerge, from there we'd make our way to the pub for the afternoon. Lee must have so enjoyed himself. So, as they say, a change is as good as a rest and for Deb and Lee I don't think it could come too soon. So while Pete George and the Fishpool team joined forces down at the Transparent Club, the Peel carried on sadly doing very well without me. I attempted to be a better husband and Dad. Sometimes I'd catch Deb looking forlornly at my son Lee and I suppose I had a good idea what was going through her mind.

The thing was from day one we'd been trying for a baby and as the years passed it was becoming a worry. On visiting the doctor he'd advised, after tactfully explaining I wasn't the world's most potent man, the members of my sperm gang preferring the backstroke, to wear loose fitting trackies and pants and eat plenty of foods containing zinc. If it helps it helps! Well eventually it did help. It took a while but when Deb announced she was pregnant we were both ecstatic and when her time came and we'd reached the days the Dad was allowed in, I experienced a cocktail of emotions. When the baby's head appeared I couldn't help but touch it. There was a streak of white hair amongst the jet black. Absentmindedly I said to Deb it's got a Mallen streak on account of I knew not yet the sex of the baby.

The pushing went on until finally this world was gifted a perfect little girl. My emotions got the better of me, I became incoherent. I'd secretly hoped for a girl. Daddy's girl and all that. I honestly thought I was going to burst I was so happy. Deb, who'd worked so hard to fetch our little girl into this world, took a well earned rest while I stared, frightened to take my eyes off my little girl. Megan would be her name. Months before we'd watched the Thorn Birds and I'd fallen in love with Rachel Ward who played Megan. The next day me and a collection of mine and Debs folks made our way to the maternity department at Townley's Hospital in Farnworth (now Bolton Royal). After helping Deb get ready for her departure I made a point of giving the two young midwives who delivered Megan a very large box of chocolates and a real heartfelt thank you.

It was already agreed that if we were blessed with kids Deb would take 12 months off work. We both agreed this was a must for the child's well-being. During these twelve months I would make myself available for any overtime plus, if any of my customers needed any jobs such as decorating doing, then I was their man. It didn't make up for the loss of Deb's wage but we managed. There was a slight worry around the situation with our dog Blue. Blue was the Alsatian collie cross that I'd bought off Bas Cowgill in The Peel one Sunday afternoon two years earlier. Blue was an absolute darling. Named after the bloodhound in the film 'Cool Hand Luke' before Blue we had two goldfish Fred and Wilma. Each day after work as I entered the kitchen where they resided, never once did either of them show any emotion at my appearance. Now with Blue he'd shake with excitement so much he'd practically levitate. He loved the two of us and showed it every day. A trait to enrich any life. What a character he was. Because of Megan's arrival, we prayed he'd show no sign of jealousy.

One incident stands out. Around two weeks before 'Bommy night' me and Deb with Megan in tow went shopping. We left Blue in the rear yard as Deb had washed the kitchen floor. We decided to shop at the Safeway store just up the road and were gone just over an hour. On returning we were shocked to find Blue sat in the little kitchen, a small single brick room extended from the main kitchen. Upon opening the door Blue sheepishly looked up, slowly wagging his tail. The outside door had acquired a hole around a foot in diameter and incredibly the pieces of hardboard that had been chewed off were placed in a neat pile at the side of where Blue was sat shaking now. For a while we just stared and tried to make sense of the scene. After coming to our senses we remembered on leaving the house hearing fireworks and commenting that it was a bit early. So the picture became clear. We could hardly chastise Blue after he'd been frightened out of his wits by fireworks and seeking shelter in his home. Well what's done is done. After patching the door I made a mental note to acquire a new door.

This is where fate took a hand. At this time I happened to be working at our Ramsbottom office on Bridge Street. The final part of my round took me to Peel Brow, a very steep road lined with solid stone Victorian houses they might have been Tudor). The following morning after the Blue incident I was delivering there, I noticed one house near the summit was being renovated on the front garden of this house had been thrown a rear door that looked in decent condition to me. On inquiring about the door I was informed I could take it, no charge. After thanking the owner I decided the following morning I would come armed with a tape measure; providing the doors dimensions weren't smaller than I needed I'd ask a mate to pick it up for me.

So picture the scene, me the postman standing over the door that lay flat on the front lawn, having measured the length and the width all I needed to know was whether the door was solid or the cheaper hardboard version which was still gracing my rear door frame. Well how do I find out if the door is solid or not? Of course. Knock on it! So there I was, bag over shoulder as I stooped down to administer the knock. At that very moment a van pulls up alongside the house with around four young fellas crammed in the front. Through the open window came a shout of "There's no fu**er in. From my crouched position, shocked, I just stared at them which seemed to increase their giddiness. As comprehension dawned on me I saw the funny side too.

By the way that door was installed on the rear frame for many years. Strangely enough my front door was retrieved from the back of a stream that ran past the front of the Florence Nightingale hospital just off Buller Street. The house was filled with furnishings acquired from friends and family members. Recycling was ingrained in the Kavanagh psyche. A couple of things I wouldn't skimp on were tea bags and coffee. We enjoy our brews. And the bed; a good night's sleep is essential.

A nice surprise was a phone call out of the blue from my old mate Phil Hartley who was running Elton Fold with the evergreen George Bennet his second in command. Phil was telling me himself and George decided the two players they needed at that time were myself and the fella I've already stated in these pages as the best amateur player Bury has produced Dave Wolfenden (Wolfy). How could I turn a chance like that down having only played alongside the mystical Wolfy once? The chance of doing so on a weekly basis was too tempting. I've already gone on at length about Wolfy's attributes, he also possessed that bull dog spirit the one ingredient that can raise us lesser mortals to an above average level.

It tends to be at the most testing times we look to these players. It was always semi-finals with me, nerves at these times fetched me almost to the point of collapse. Why I reacted so badly I'll never know. But as the referee was about to start the game I'd look around at my team mates and the heart players, the lads who come what may would give their all were to me a real comfort. I remember discussing my nerve problem with our Pat. His reaction was sobering to say the least. Pat said "you don't know how lucky you are to take part in semi's and finals" and promptly walked off. After some personal soul searching I realised sadly, although our Pat was a decent, very enthusiastic player, he'd never played in a semi never mind a final. His last team Tottington St. Annes every season went cap in hand to the next.

These lads were a lesson to us all. They knew they would always be strangers to silverware. They could live with that, they were just happy to be there. One day the situation arose where my Saturday team, Prestwich Heys were without a match. I decided to watch St. Annes, our Pat asking me to fetch my boots just in case. They were playing Totty Utd. at Town Meadow. As it turned out St. Annes were a man short so I took to the pitch. My team mates seemed to me very relaxed and looking forward to the imminent game.

In the changing room before the game I was struck by the sheer enthusiasm of these lads. Jokes were thrown around such as "no hugging and kissing if we get a corner, it's embarrassing". Well turned out we did better than win a corner, we actually won the match 3–2. The lads played like heroes every last one of them. It was an inspiring afternoon and once more impressed on me no team has a divine right to win, and here was another example of effort and determination triumphing over a more illustrious opponent. You'd have thought we'd won the league. In the Dungeon after the match the St. Annes lads were flying, the party atmosphere continued all afternoon into the evening. To the victor the spoils. This great set of lads had their day. How long it would be till their next celebration was anyone's guess. One thing's for sure, their lads would turn out in strength each week of the season.

Shaggy Dog Story

Bury Post Office sports day was to be held at Elton Lib. club New George Street. These events were great sport allowing us posties to show our prowess at such games as snooker, darts and crown green bowling which I particularly enjoyed.

The afternoon would fly by and after a short speech announcing and congratulating the winners, myself Robin Lomax and the legendary Bury fans and all round sports fans the Edge brothers, Barry and Dave decided we'd make our way to the Dusty Miller at the junction of Tottington Road and Walshaw Road. On our way down we called in the Pleasant View at the bottom of Totty Road. We were greeted by some mates neither of us had seen for a while and well you know, 'Yesterday's Wine' and all that. When we finally made our way to the Dusty lets say we were exceptionally merry. We had a rare old time in the Dusty, I think we'd have had a rare old time in the middle of a ploughed field the condition we were in.

The condition of Robin was declining by the minute. He'd gone from being the hard but lovable fella we knew and loved to someone who was struggling to utter a word and wore an expression similar to a little boy who'd pooh'd his pants. Barry, sensing the deterioration of our mate informed me and Dave he would see Robin home to his house on the Woodhill Estate, saying he'd meet us in the 'Help Me Thro' soon as he'd got Robin safely home. Well I'm guessing it must have been an hour later before Barry's beaming face appeared in the vault of the 'Help Me Thro'. "You won't believe it." "Believe what?" Barry commenced to relay the story to me and David; after leaving us he was helping Robin on the short walk along Woodhill Road to his home when Robin suddenly stopped, took hold of a fence post with both hands, head bowed and commenced as we say "shouting for Huey". All Barry could do was what any good mate could do which was to pat Robin's back while uttering the time honoured words "get it all up, you'll feel better." After an extra hard lurch of Robin's stomach his new dentures flew from the comfortable but busy place that was Robin's mouth onto the vomit soaked paving stone straddled by Robin's feet.

Incredibly, at the exact moment, Robin was attempting to retrieve his beloved dentures a passing Woodhill dingo had them in its jaws and was off. As Robin screamed incoherent noises, gallant Barry took up the chase. Barry said after chasing the dog up and down Litchfield Drive he'd given up the chase as it headed at pace in the direction of the Burrs. He finished the tale by telling me and Dave his parting words to Robin which were "don't worry Robin, how many dogs on Woodhill will be running round with a smile like a Cheshire cat?" at which we all cracked up, then ordered another pint.

Life at Bury sorting office was full of those sort of scenarios which, together with the absence of the monotony that accompanied my days on the production lines, made my working life as a Bury postie an absolute joy. Over the coming years hardly an inch of Bury or Ramsbottom escaped my footfall, the latter containing some lovely and very interesting areas, my first visit to Strongstry in Stubbins Village was a real treat. You could film a period drama within its borders, the lovely parish church of St Phillip and the steam train passing in the background made a lovely picture. I like Ramsbottom, it maintains an old world villagey feel. My sister Mary has resided in Shutterworth for several decades now, her partner Tom Wolfenden comes from farming stock. Although a breed on their own I've always enjoyed Tom's company. A real man of the soil, he enjoys nothing more than setting out with his dog Jug and spending many hours traipsing over the hills around Ramsbottom and surrounding areas. He's a wise old sage and as honest as they come.

A few years back his two sons Steven and David asked their Dad if they could purchase a small plot of land at the side of Tom's Bye Road home with a view to building two houses to accommodate themselves and their families. A token purchase price was agreed on and with spring in the air the two lads wasted no time in setting about their task in hand, both having building experience the bulk of the work would be managed by themselves. The things they weren't qualified for such as wiring, gas, etc. friends promised to help with. The day came round for them to begin digging the foundations. Not usually the most inspiring of tasks but boy were they in for a shock. As they began digging they were surprised to find large cut stones just below the surface. Thinking the few stones they'd hoisted from the soil would come in handy they stacked them neatly at the side of the gate. They couldn't believe their luck when late that evening they were still finding stones by the score. The next day the same and the next. Staggeringly the two lads recovered enough stone from the now very large hole to erect two fine three-storey houses with a garden wall to boot. It would be interesting to know the history of the original buildings, no one seems too sure not even Tom himself but if you're ever on your way to Fisherman's Retreat take a minute to view the two houses that have risen Phoenix-like to stand proud once again on their original birthplace.

I'm a regular visitor to our Mary and Tom's home at Bye Road. Mary now being the matriarch of the Kavanagh family, homage must and must willingly be paid. The old house is a place of peace and tranquillity. Mary and Tom's Vera and Jack relationship I always find very amusing. They've raised their kids and all but the youngest has flown the nest. And secretly I think they both hope it's a while before he follows suit.

On the football front the 90–91 season would prove fruitful. This season would find me playing in Elton Fold reserves but really enjoying my football alongside some cracking younger lads such as Mark Bentley, Adie Newbury, Phil Turner, Ste Bellis and for balance a couple of old heads in the form of Dave Doran (Dicky) Andy Lindsay and myself, led by our wonderful player manager the incomparable Phil Hartley. Playing some great football we would lift the Bolton Combination Division 2 cup. I missed playing alongside Wolfy in the first team but I was enjoying this. This was the year Deb's brother Ste Coffee would make his debut joining me in the reserves. Ste had just finished a season playing for Bolton Wanderers reserves, any chance we got me and his old fella Jim would take the trip to Burnden Park to watch him. It was a comedown but Ste wasn't the sort to dwell on the past, unlike some. He certainly gave us in the reserves a boost. Unsurprisingly it wasn't long before the first team came knocking. He settled in quickly and became a very popular squad member.

All was well till January when amateur football in Bury would be in mourning following the untimely death of one of the town's real characters and a fine experienced footballer Mike Miniero (Mini) playing for his Sunday team Raven FC Mike collapsed and died in the arms of his manager Walter Duckworth. We lost a special man. A few weeks prior to this fateful event I'd been nagging Mini to sell me a short red leather jacket he wore. Being of Italian descent Mini wasn't short on style and I loved that jacket. Just before Christmas whilst training at Elton school gym I was paired up with Mini.

An incident while we were exercising, which at the time I hardly noticed, would return to my mind sharply a couple of weeks later. Phil Hartley who was training us that night asked for 20 press ups, while your partner counted out. I was pretty good at press ups and Mini's shout of 20 came sooner than I'd thought. So now it was Mini's turn. He looked apprehensive. He began but straight away he just didn't look at all comfortable. His movements were slow and staggered after completing only six. He remained flat on the deck and looked distinctly flustered. "You OK Mini?" "Yeah, I just struggle at press ups." I should have known then there was something wrong. In the showers afterwards I began my nagging about the jacket. Mini gave in. "Give me a tenner" he said and that night I went home wearing Mini's jacket which to this day is hanging in my pantry. It's a little tight now but when I wear it, it's with pride and fond memories.

As already mentioned, this was the season us in the Elton Fold reserve side would find ourselves in the final of the league cup on the day of the game in order for me to have time to chill out which was my usual pre match ritual, I decided I'd get a 'wriggle on' and rush to finish my round, never easy for me. Being a sociable fella I enjoyed a chat to the point where an ex-girlfriend made the comment "I don't know about kissing the Blarney Stone, I think Eamon was necking with it." Very droll. Anyway things were going well. I'd avoided any chit-chat. I entered the Co-op on Ainsworth Road to collect my last bag and proceeded to fly down Horbury Drive, up and down garden paths as fast as my legs would take me. Then disaster, as I was rushing down one path the strap from my delivery pouch snagged on the brick gate column. With the speed I was travelling and the sheer weight in my overloaded bag the top third of the column came crashing down. For a moment I just stared at the debris, trying to convince myself it wasn't my fault.

All was quiet, no-one was roused by the crash of the bricks. The thought to make myself scarce I confess passed through my mind but, deep down, I knew it would come back to haunt me. As sometimes it does, fate played its hand. At the bottom of the street workmen were beginning the building of the new houses on the Old Alderman Smith school site. I rushed down to the site. Timidly I asked one of the bricklayers if he could spare a little cement. The guy was obliging and filled the polythene bag I held open for him. I dismissed the thought of asking him for a loan of his trowel as pushing my luck. After thanking him profusely I made my way to a house facing the scene of my accident which was owned by a very agreeable chap. My luck was in as he had a trowel, obviously I had to let him in on my plan to remedy the damage before anyone was the wiser. Promising to return the towel forthwith, he closed his door and I set about my task. With my speed and unexpected dexterity, accomplishing said task pleased me no end.

After knocking on his door and placing the trowel in my good man's hand I turned and we both stared at the repaired column. With not a little pride I said to the good man "not bad for a bloke who's never laid a brick in his life, eh?" He looked at me and smiling said "it's pretty straight, I'll give you that but shouldn't it be the same size as the other column? Stunned I stared at my imagined masterpiece. It stood a good four inches taller than its twin. All I could do was mumble 'How'? Why? How's that come about?' The good man then asked me "you did knock the old mortar off, didn't you?" Staring at him, not a word to say, he knew the answer. I informed him I couldn't hang about any longer as I had a big game on. He whispered in my ear with a sneaky grin "you don't say anything, neither will I." On that note I patted him on the shoulder and set off at speed to finish my round with a little more care. Years later 'Uneven Towers' as I named them, still grace the entrance to the house and never a word said to me.

During my nomadic periods in the past (not having my own round) these times were a good insight into the varying qualities of life experienced by the residents of our fair town of Bury. I know to use the term 'our town' seems strange written by a resident of the town of Bolton. The explanation is simple: economics. I feel the need to say I've enjoyed my time here in Bolton. My neighbours are good solid folk and to say we are on a main road, opposite a pub, it's pretty quiet. But although my body resides in Bolton, my heart and mind will always belong to Bury. Sometimes it's not easy to explain your love for a thing or a place. Obviously its the people that makes a place good or bad to inhabit. I can honestly say the majority of Bury folk I've chatted to at length express views and demonstrate qualities of a breed of folk who believe in the greater good, even to the point of self-detriment to achieve it. Although I accept the majority of these views belong to let's say the more mature folk, the hope is their experience and wise counsel will catch in some of the ears of our younger folk.

The Middle Ground

I've always believed that money is no guaranteed route to contentment. During my life to date I have never had savings and never more than a couple of hundred pounds in my account, yet in the main I'm a contented and happy person. However, to stand back and take a detached summary of my experience working in all the different districts within Bury's borders I have found the most content folk occupying the middle ground. Not the folk with the huge houses, a set of top of the range cars to go with their jet set lives and all the stress of maintaining their lifestyles. Nor those at the bottom of the food chain where their shortage of funds can mean each day's a struggle.

Elton Fold, my round for many years, begins at the bottom of Ainsworth Road, in length goes as far as Chantler's school, and in width to Holcombe Avenue and Guardian Angels school. The majority of folk on Elton Fold weren't rich or poor. As a rule their moods were upbeat. So it seems if you had a choice a wise one would be to take the middle path. It seems, as I suspected, this is not a new discovery. Daniel Defoe in his wonderful book 'Robinson Crusoe' had the young Crusoe being advised by his father to seek the middle station in life as this was the least taxing, and therefore contentment was easily acquired. Robinson Crusoe was written nearly 300 years ago, makes you wonder.

In this respect I feel lucky as a postman for Royal Mail; caviar wasn't on the menu but then again neither was bread and water. Me and Deb made sure our bills were paid and usually there was enough for an occasional night out. Neither of us being motivated by money, we felt lucky.

Driving Test

This situation would be tested a little when Deb informed me she was with child again. I was really made up, Deb seemed a little less made up. We'd agreed before Megan was born Deb would take a year off work agreeing it would be good for the child and Deb. But obviously it would put a strain on our finances. I'd learned at work that they had a provision whereby they'd supply driving lessons free of charge providing that once you had your license you'd agree to drive one of their vans for a minimum of a month. The drivers were on slightly more money than a footman but more importantly they tended to be asked to do more overtime. So it came to pass, after many lessons, that a day was named for my driving test.

The time for my test would be 3pm on a Friday afternoon. This left it tight as my pre-test lesson was 2pm and with me being just about the slowest postman in Bury, was cutting it fine. As luck would have it that Friday, us footmen and girls were swamped with mail. In order for me to make sure I'd finish early, my natural inclinations to enjoy a chat with any customers at large would have to be harnessed to the point of, to my mind, almost antisocial. Needs must. Why is it on the rare occasions I needed to get a wriggle on all the customers I bumped into seemed insistent for me to remain still while they regaled me with tales of mankind's imminent extinction if he didn't change his ways, wayward kids and the price of butter. In normal circumstances I really enjoyed this part of my job but today its my driving test and they should know by the way I'm shuffling my feeT I need to get on. I couldn't be so ignorant as to say I must get on. Instead I'd step up the shuffling and dusting imaginary cobwebs from my clothing. Well I got done on time and did really well on my 2pm lesson. As you'd imagine, I felt quietly confident while waiting for my examiner.

I was completely unprepared for what followed when he arrived. After taking my place in the driver's seat all was well but when the examiner who, by the way, seemed a nice enough fella, uttered the word 'proceed' my breathing became erratic and I couldn't keep my feet from shaking. The examiner wisely asked me to pull over. He then told me to take deep breaths and try to relax. We must have been stopped around ten minutes before we set off again. Mentally I was on a 'wing and a prayer'. I felt physically ill. The last straw was stopping at the lights outside the George and Dragon, opposite Fairfield Hospital. As the lights turned to green I released the hand-brake and rolled back into what looked to me a brand new Mondeo. The driver of the Mondeo will have my everlasting thanks as he calmly got out of his car and whispered in my ear "forget it, there's no damage and good luck on your next test."

I think he'd took one look at my ashen face and understood the situation. By this time I was feeling so emotional I almost hugged him. With tears welling, me and the examiner switched places and he drove us safely back to the driving centre at Smith Street. There would be two more test days waiting in the future, the second following very similar lines as the first. The lessons leading up to my third would be instructed by my friend and work colleague Paul Sharman, a smashing lad and not a bad footballer. Paul had passed all his exams and was now a qualified instructor. With me his patience would be sorely tested.

Two days before my test he informed me he was taking me for a mock test. Holding an official test form we set off around Bury and Ramsbottom. As we finally pulled up outside my home Paul turned to me and said "Eamon there's too many errors to go through in this life. It's too late to put the test back. It's basically damage limitation. See you Friday, 2pm." Yes, another Friday 3pm test, things didn't bode well.

My mate Kenny said he would do my last bag for me which would guarantee me an early finish. I was home for 12.30 and decided an hour relaxing on my bed going over my shortcomings would maybe help matters. At the time I was minding my niece's Yorkshire Terrier dog Alfie, Alfie was a little darling. Blue, our dog, thankfully loved Alfie as well and to be sure they were good company for each other. On opening the front door I received a lovely greeting. After a while Blue settled in the kitchen, Alfie on the other hand wouldn't leave my side. As a treat I gave Alfie some sardines I thought he'd enjoy. Enjoy them he did, he nearly took the pattern off the plate. After deciding on my meditational siesta I made my way to the bedroom with Alfie following close behind, realizing I couldn't lock him out and relax as he would bark to come in and join me, I closed the door and Alfie and me settled into our own thoughts on the bed. Me going over things like reverse parking, keeping steady speed, using my mirrors, all the things I was weak on. Alfie's thoughts were probably on the cute little Yorkie next door.

At this time I was mentally attempting to relax and prepare myself for the test to come. Thoughts like how important it is compared to, say, a serious illness and that I could always do it again. I was thinking like this when there was what I can only describe as a small explosion in the room followed by the foulest smell. Enough to say – no more sardines for Alfie. I'd just finished cleaning up when Paul knocked on the door. I grabbed my jacket and told Alfie to cross his legs till I got back. As I drove off Paul told me he thought the root of my problem was plain and simple nerves and because of this he'd been to the chemist and bought me a new remedy which had just come on the market especially for folk like me who he believed to be a competent driver but hindered by nerves. The idea was to spray three squirts under the tongue. On reaching the Smith Street centre I told Paul I was just whipping to the loo. On reaching the cubicle I took out the remedy spray, unscrewed the top and drank down more than half of the contents. On returning to the car Paul said he'd see me later and to just do my best. After Paul left me and I was waiting for my examiner, nerves got the best of me and I downed the rest of the bottle.

As the examiner took his place in the passenger seat I thought I'd better take my feet of the dashboard. Only kidding! But I felt that relaxed, I don't know what was in that bottle but I'll sing its praises forever. After about 20 five minutes of driving I hadn't done anything really stupid. As a result I could feel myself getting really excited which in a way is as bad as really nervous. So incredibly I engaged the examiner in conversation and struck gold, he really enjoyed football. So there I was, driving round the outskirts of Bury like an old pro, discussing the beautiful game with my examiner. As we pulled into Smith Street I couldn't even pretend I could describe to you how I felt.

Paul had already told me he'd informed our workmates I'd no chance this time but he'd get me through my next test. The only words I could use to come near how I felt was absolute bliss. If I was any judge of character this man at my side had made his mind up halfway through the test and I knew what he had decided. As we entered the car park at Smith Street the examiner asked me to reverse into a parking space. As I was attempting the maneuver I caught a glimpse of Paul watching intently from the window of the test centre. Needless to say I made a bit of a hash of the reverse parking, on the second attempt I just managed the maneuver. A worried looking Paul wearily made his way over to us. I looked back at him with a similar look. Making sure my window was down a little my examiner turned to me and said these immortal words "Well Mr. Kavanagh, I'm happy to tell you, you've passed. And I must add, a most enjoyable ride!" The look on Paul's face was priceless, his next action was even more so. He proceeded to jump up and down the car park like Skippy on hot coals at the same time "yahoo-ing" like a demented rodeo rider. The expression on my examiner's face said it all. Paul was certainly acting strange but then again he had no knowledge of what had gone before.

So here I was, armed with a brand new driving license and a choice to make. Would I carry on working for Royal Mail as a footman or a driver? For better or for worse I decided to stay as a footman, coming to this decision with the help of whispered advice to take notice how unfit most of our drivers were. This certainly seemed the case and, to be honest, I didn't trust myself not to end up the same, so the decision to carry on doing what I loved was an easy one. The move was only about money anyway and money versus health is no contest. As it turned out during Deb's pregnancy with our second child I managed to acquire enough overtime for us to get along just fine.

When Ethan, our son, was born in early December, we couldn't have asked for a better Christmas present. But strangely Deb seemed a little subdued. I put it down to the baby blues and hoped it would pass. I know I put her through hell when Mum and Dad died, leaving her, coming back, leaving again. I knew I'd done some damage but naively I hoped time would be the cure-all. I made the decision, after long consideration, to ignore the situation with Deb, not always the wisest path. This would be a time when my decision-making would be erratic to say the least. Before this season finished I would leave Elton Fold and join up with Dave Morris, a guy I've got a lot of time for. Dave at this time was managing Clitheroe, a lovely little club I really enjoyed my brief time there. We did well and won the league, to my surprise on the last day of the season Dave had a quiet word with me, he told me he'd decided to return the following season to manage Radcliffe Borough and would I join him? He informed me he'd already had a word with my old mucker Kenny Bellis and a few other lads I'd already enjoyed playing alongside.

So that was that. The following season would see my return to Stainton Park. If I'm honest I was enjoying my Sunday football more than Saturdays. Our Pat and Les had assembled some of the finest players I've played with, the fact they were all, and I mean all, good lads just added to the pot. Some of the afternoons we had in the back room of the Peel! Well sometimes I'd wished I could have bottled them and saved them for leaner times. There was Paddy Mac our leader. To get Paddy laughing wasn't an easy task but after being plied with enough drink, he'd be chuckling along with the rest of us. The team was full of lads who didn't mind, even encouraged self deprecation. I loved it, no one will convince me there's anything better than a natural high. And that's how I felt in their company – high. The humour was never aggressive, no one went too far. Rossy would accept the stick he received in good heart, he'd take the blame for anything that went wrong with our game plan, whether he was in the vicinity or not.

The thing was there was so much talent in the side, very little did go wrong. That was until one fatal April day in Rochdale. We were playing a local team under the dubious name of 'Tim Bobbin'. That was enough for me, who's going to be afraid of a team named 'Tim Bobbin'? This was the quarter final of the North West Counties Cup. We had a strong side out that day. I say a strong side, four of our regulars were out but their places were filled with competent lads. Derick Makin made his debut in this game. A big strong uncompromising full back, Dave Jowett came in between the sticks. Paddy, Rossy, our Michael, Willy 'Big Bird', Mick Brooks, Butch McManus and Trevor Lewis and myself took the field in confident mood.

As I took my position on the right wing which put me next to their dugout, I noticed my old teammate from my Prestwich Heys days Micky Rae who was subbing for them. "Hi Micky, how you doin?" "Fine Eamon you?" "Fine, looking forward to a good game." "Nowt down for you today cocker. Damage limitation." I was a little taken aback by this comment, why was he so confident, he knew nothing about us. He obviously didn't realise who we were, we're Peel FC for God's sake, one of the best Sunday teams to ever come out of the fair town of Bury. What's going through his mind? Well we'll just have to see, won't we? Almost straight from the kick-off we won a corner on the left, Butch took the corner which he whipped in avoiding the near post, incredibly the ball came through a ruck of players and arrived at my feet at the far post. I had the simple task of side-footing the ball into the net. 1–0 to us. Fetch it on.

Less than 15 minutes later I ran between two central defenders to meet a bouncing ball perfectly with my head to send it sailing over their oncoming 'keeper to sweetly settle into the net. As I took my place for the restart I couldn't help looking over to Mickey Rae in their dugout and mouthing to him 'Easy!" Mickey just smiled back saying "Eamon, Eamon, you'll see!"What is going on in that lad's head? Sadly I was to find out sooner than I thought. In the space of 15 minutes they hit us with six cracking goals. Up to this time their two big cumbersome-looking forwards appeared to pose no threat. How wrong can you be? Between them they added another four top drawer goals. This would be a defeat still talked about by anyone concerned to this day. The saying goes, if you want to ruin an ex Peel FC player's night out, just mention 'Tim Bobbin'.

After we returned to The Peel to lick our wounds. This would be the one occasion when laughter was in short supply, anyone looking as if they might break into a giggle got one look from Paddy Mac and it was enough to suppress it at birth. Even at social get-togethers, where happily many of us original players still enjoy each others company and will get together at the drop of hat, you'll often hear the words "Don't mention Tim Bobbin" a direct take off of "Don't mention the war". After all these years we can now laugh about it.

Wrong Again

My friendship with my mate John Saxon (Sacko) had an unpromising birth. I'd known Sacko before I actually met him, as his larger than life character went before him. Anything for a laugh, loud and a drinker, I appreciated the fun side of these characters but in a one to one situation I never felt too comfortable. I always felt like I'd have to spend the time in their company doing or saying crazy things otherwise you'd be labelled boring. So when I heard he'd moved into a house on the next block to me, I honestly felt gutted. It hadn't been long since Deb had informed me she was leaving with the kids and even though we maintained a good relationship, I was still coming to terms with the situation. The truth was the last thing I wanted was someone like Sacko popping round regularly. Every knock on the door I'd sneak a look through the gap in the curtains in case it was Sacko. One day it was Sacko and I take no pride in admitting I pretended to be out. The second and third time he called I kept up the pretense.

As time went by I honestly felt he'd given up till one evening I'd called over to the petrol station as I'd run out of milk and was making my way back when I felt a tap on my shoulder, looked round and yes, there he stood, larger than life, grinning like a Cheshire cat. "Making a brew then?" "Yeah. You fancy one?" "Go on then, ha ha!" Shite! Well what could I do, sometimes there's no room for maneuver. So the supposed new bane of my life entered my inner sanctum, my peaceful home was about to be violated by a 'good time Charlie' who frankly I wasn't in the mood for. So reluctantly I went through the ritual of famous Lancashire hospitality and 'brewed up', at the same time my mind racing, hoping to come up with something to keep this visit short. When I entered the living room from the kitchen Sacko had picked up a book a friend had thought would do me good and was quietly scanning the introduction. After passing him his brew and saying "it's a great book," Sacko asked if he could borrow it. I told him as the friend who borrowed it said there was no rush to return it, I didn't see any harm but made Sacko promise to look after it. The book in question was 'The Road Less Travelled' by Scott Peck. I told Sacko that before this book, the last book I read was at junior school and it was....... Just as I was about to answer Sacko says "Wind in the Willows". My jaw dropped and I stared at him. It was my last book too, to which we both cracked up laughing. At this point my memory reminded me 'actually the last book you read was Wuthering Heights'. I let the fact pass.

We spent the next few hours discussing the book and many other subjects, washed down with many cups of 'Rosy Lee'. And, to my immense surprise, I closed the door behind Sacko at around midnight and realised I'd really enjoyed myself. So much for my character judgement. At that time Sacko was driving for the company 'Chubb'. A bad error of judgement on his part would change all that. While leaving the Wellington Pub on Bolton Road late one night a little worse for wear, instead of flagging a taxi for the couple of miles trip home, stupidly he got into his work's van and set off vaguely in the direction of home. Inevitably he was stopped by the police and breathalysed and the van and his job went up the Swanny. This was Sacko living up to his public image. But I knew this was something that would silence the laughter. After all, he'd just took on his first mortgage. He'd been stupid but I felt for him. I know he was gutted.

One night soon after I saw him down and informed him I'd had a word with Debs dad Jim Coffey who was a foreman at a firm down Astley bridge named Indispention who were a small engineering firm. Jim had had a word with the boss who agreed to give Sacko a start the following Monday. Sacko was made up. I told him "before you get too excited the work's boring and the money's bobbins". But it will keep the roof over your head till something better comes along. So we had another brew and I kicked him out, told him I wanted an early night as I'd done two rounds that day. Eventually Sacko was successful in seeking employment with Royal Mail and after a short stint in Bolton acquired a transfer to Bury which was grand as he only lived up the road from me and he owned a car so my lift to work was guaranteed.

This was probably just as well as on a personal level I wasn't in great shape. After long heart-rending talks with Deb she stayed adamant that she was leaving. She reminded me that after my Mum and Dad's passing, how horrible I had been to her. Deb then went on relaying some of these things. It wasn't easy listening. Without going into detail the fact she was talking to me was unbelievable. I was in pain and I took it out on Deb. How Pathetic. My desperate pleadings and promises of change went unheeded. I don't think I've ever felt so low. The house seemed like an empty shell with me feeling the same way. My way of handling it was to shun visits from friends including family.

Seeking solace in a bottle of whiskey and playing sad country songs all night ended up with me becoming an emotional wreck and half the time not bothering with the stairs. After weeks of this, inevitably work suffered to the point where I ignored Sacko's banging on the door and hollering through the letter box. I honestly didn't give a damn. I was enjoying my misery. I deserved it. Something had to give and it came in the shape of my lovely brother Michael. Me and Michael had over the years become closer than even brothers had a right to, he embodied all the things I admired in a good human being: honesty, thoughtfulness, humility and he enjoyed nothing more than ensuring other people's enjoyment. Completely selfless. He took time off work and spent a week listening to my woes. We both cried and drank whisky. By the end of the week we were singing classic Irish songs, 'Dublin in the Rare Auld Times' 'The Fields of

Athenry' and Michael's favourite 'Seven Drunken Nights', with a couple of verses added! On the last night we both made vows that in time of need we would always be there for one another and in memory of Mum and Dad we would make the most of the life we had left. A vow that will never be broken. There have been times since that time that our roles were reversed and I only hope and pray I was as much a comfort to Michael as he was to me.

2000 – From Elton Fold to Elton Vale

What a momentous year for my old club Elton Fold. Work had finished on their new home which bordered my round at Elton Vale Road. On viewing their new sports ground the word I used again and again was 'fabulous' and it was. A fine cricket pitch, lovely tennis courts, rounders area. Without doubt the best pitch in Bury, only surpassed by the hallowed turf of Gigg Lane. And to top it all a cracking club house sporting classy portraits of former loyal servants, now committee members.

After Royal Mail football team folded, my Saturdays would be spent watching Elton's 1st & 2nd teams, whoever happened to be at home, being greeted with "How arrti!" just so you knew you were in the company of mature Bury folk. Then gazing out across the pitch in its lovely setting along with lads like Dave Wolfy, Dicky Doran, Paul Rigby and Phil Hartley. Knowing we were all thinking the same. Running out on a pitch like that along with our younger legs. Ah well. It's lovely to be involved with a well run amateur club like Elton Vale. I suppose to the fact you knew everyone involved with the club from the groundsman Jim Murray, the Manager Phil Hartley to the tea ladies, Margaret and Shirley.

I can't pretend I'm a cricket fan but on a sunny day, with a pint of Guinness in hand the sight of our cricket team competing against the backdrop of Holcombe Hill and surrounding area takes some beating. Even with facilities like these it's not easy running a football team. Standing on the sidelines by the dugout with our Pat, Michael and my mate Kenny, week in, week out, we witness the ups and downs of the manager's lot. We celebrate with his successes and show empathy on the bad days. Incredibly Vale find it hard to keep hold of their players. With their facilities this appeared to many of us fans a total mystery.

We realise today's youngsters have more diversions than us older lads had. "There's not the same passion today" is a comment you will often hear. This may be so but somehow I doubt it. Football is still the greatest game on the planet. And the chance to actually play the game you love rather than watch it surely still tips the scales. Even with Phil Hartley at the helm, a lovely well respected character in Bury's amateur scene, players are still drifting which must be so frustrating for Phil and the other lads. But the Vale are our team in good or bad times. Me and my brothers, Kenny and the rest, will be there every week because they're our team. I'd hate to think we'd be so fickle as to be good time supporters. So "come on the Vale". How does the song go "Even the bad times are good."

The Days of Wine and More Wine

After the demise of Bury Royal Mail FC me, Kenny and Sacko decided Friday after work should be given over to our favourite pastime of drinking red wine and putting the world to rights. A book was purchased which would be used as a ledger to mark the different wines. They would be marked simply from one to 10. The book would be called "Eamon, Kenny and Sacko's Not Too Serious Wine Book." During the three years we had our wine nights it would be fair to say a couple of times we ended up in bad shape.

These nights were held in my kitchen. We'd be drinking the fruit of the vine, discussing some subject that had taken our interest and in the background country music, usually Johnny Cash, played as we all loved him. At other times It'd be Irish, mostly because Sacko loved dancing to it. I reckon I can do a half decent jig but Sacko took it to new levels. And, to be honest, I really liked his style, so much, I ended up copying it. It involves the classic heel-toe alternate leg style but with Sacko everything was exaggerated, from a raised position behind him each leg would swing forward into a high kick. I couldn't help but get up and join him. Then usually Kenny, suffering already from arthritic knees, would join in, in time with "The Irish Rover".

Looking back I can't believe how we managed in my small kitchen but manage we did. On the hot evenings we'd shed our tops. After our exertions we found candlelight relaxing and more conducive with good banter. One night after a couple of bottles each Kenny took an orange from my large fruit bowl and tossed it at me about chest high. On instinct I chested the orange, flicked it up with my knee and executed a perfect strike which sent said orange at great speed to the ceiling. My ceilings happen to have that Artex effect gained by a twisting action, the result being sharp spiky patterns. The orange embedded itself on this surface which, probably because of the drink we'd consumed, really tickled us. You can guess where the rest of the contents of the fruit bowl ended up.

At 4am the next morning, bleary-eyed I stumbled down the stairs and into my kitchen. Fumbling for the kettle I was startled from being hit on the head by the remains of a decomposing apple that at that moment chose to leave its place embedded on the Artex ceiling. I'd had my own personal Isaac Newton moment. The Chinese whispers collecting on the grapevine at work we found hilarious. Turns out me, Kenny and Sacko were to be found any Friday night stripped naked, jumping over a candle placed in the middle of the room with 'Great Balls of Fire' playing in the background. They will have their fun. Undaunted, our wine-fuelled Fridays continued.

By this time me and Sacko were heavily into reading books, sometimes up to two a week. Our reading material was varied but for some reason I leaned towards the old writers, Wilkie Collins, Hardy, Dickens, Mark Twain. No mystery really, hankering for the past is nothing new for me. I know its daft but what the heck. Kenny was our anchor man when me and Sacko rose above our stations he wasted no time in fetching us back to earth. I can't remember ever seeing Kenny leathered. Me and Sacko would sometimes end up stumbling around but Kenny always seemed in charge of his faculties.

Only once on a Saturday afternoon, after an extra drunken evening, I happened to meet Kenny's wife, the lovely Nicola on Bury Market. She stopped me and, as nicely as she could, asked me what the hell had gone on the night before. Genuinely surprised, I asked her what she meant. "I got up this morning, walked into the living room and there he was face down on the floor, spread-eagled pants round his ankles and still clutching a kebab in his right hand." Well I know I shouldn't have but I just cracked up laughing. I couldn't get the picture out of my head. Nicola just walked off shaking her head. I should have known then our days were numbered. But the end wasn't the one I'd envisaged.

One Friday in June 2003 I answered the phone in my kitchen. The wine night was already in full swing. Above the din I heard my son Lee's voice pleading for me to turn the music down. After doing that and asking the lads to quiet down for a minute, Lee informed me from this day on I'd be known as Grandad. Well I don't have to tell you we celebrated like there was no tomorrow. We all agreed we'd meet up the next night, Saturday, in our favourite pub at the time, The White Lion to wet the baby's head. Well that Saturday we had ourselves a brilliant night with our old mate Billy Stanley supplying the musical entertainment. When Joan the landlady rang the bell for last orders we were still singing our hearts out along with Billy to the old classics. Joan ran a tight ship so not long after the bell we made our way to the Two Tubs where we drank till the wee hours.

We ended the night in our favourite eating place, Rajahs, at the bottom of Bolton Road. The head man there is one of life's diamonds. We've ended up there in some states but he never took offense, he would pour us a coffee each, feed us the most delicious food, then order us a taxi to take us home. What a guy. So it was early morning when I gratefully fell into bed fully clothed bar my shoes. It was around 9am when the bedside phone rang. Mick Williams voice sounded so loud as he tried to explain he'd be at mine for 9.30am for our five-a-side match scheduled for 10am.

Before I could explain how bad I felt, Mick had said "we've a bare five, be ready," then hung up. Nothing for it. Cold shower and two strong coffees. By the time Mick beeped his horn I was out the door, kit bag in hand and an uncomfortable feeling about how I was going to get through this. We were scheduled for two matches. On the way I decided I would just have to take it easy, that's what I'd do. Well, the best laid plans and all that. I ended up running around like a chicken with no head, where the energy came from I know not. We left Coney Green school in Radcliffe with two wins under our belts and satisfied grins. I declined the boys' offer of a quick pint, figuring I'd had just about enough ale to last me a year.

Dropped at my door I decided to make a brew and some toast. It happened then; a sharp pain in my chest. The initial pain took my breath away. Thankfully not permanently, after that it was just a constant ache. So, like so many others I took an aspirin, lay on the floor with my feet up watching telly. This was the worst case of indigestion I'd ever had, obviously because of the amount of ale in my system with a curry on top. It was a week later when I mentioned it to my then girlfriend Sue. She insisted we made our way to Bardock walk-in centre in Parson's Lane.

Before I knew what was happening I was in a Fairfield hospital bed, wired up to my eyes. ECGs, blood pressure, blood samples. I was to spend three weeks in that hospital bed and as crazy as it sounds I really enjoyed it. I'd never stayed in a hospital before. Up to this time I'd enjoyed good health, football injuries apart. I'd been as fit as a fiddle. So here I was, feeling pretty fine, friends and family making daily pilgrimages to see me bearing gifts and hugs they made such a fuss of me. Brilliant nurses who couldn't do enough for me. It felt so good. Lee, Megan and Ethan didn't hide their feelings but I put them at ease, telling them how well I felt. Which I did! As the days passed I began to get to know the other patients, one fella in particular, Harry Lomas a cracking bloke. Harry was like me, a simple guy who enjoyed the simple things. We both would get real excited when meal times came round. Hospital food. What I'd heard didn't bear out. Me and Harry loved it. Harry's health problems were pretty severe, a triple bypass was waiting for him but he was an old trooper and a guy who enjoyed each day he was blessed with.

One afternoon while surrounded by a few mates and Sue, a young doctor came up to my bed and asked them all bar Sue if they wouldn't mind leaving while he had a word with me. I was pretty calm even when he pulled the curtain around the bed. His words certainly left me anything but calm. Holding Sue's hand I was stunned when the doctor told me it was bad news. Me and Sue just stared at him. I can't even recall what he said next, apart from the word damage, it was only when Sue said "Eamon" and looking to our joined hands, the sight of blood trickling down between her fingers brought me back to my senses. After apologising to Sue then being rebuffed for it because she understood totally. What a darling. After the doctor had left and our friends returned it was a little awkward, after the news I'd just received it wasn't easy to lift myself. They all understood, gave me a hug and left me and Sue to ponder this information. The thing was, I felt grand and that was good enough for me.

I set my stall out early doors. Slowing down, taking it easy, definitely wasn't in the script. The day I cannot run will probably be my last. That might seem a little cavalier, it's not that way. I simply want to carry on in the pattern I always have. Very active and a few glasses of wine along the way. Our Pat came out with a classic when I informed him of this. His reply: "If you want things to stay as they are, things will have to change." Yes Pat!

Back to Work

Life is hard. These are the opening words of the brilliant book 'The Road Less Travelled' by Scott Peck. On my first day back after my little episode, trudging up Ainsworth Road with my trolley, those words passed through my mind. My time of being mollycoddled was short and sweet; the real world came knocking with a message for me. "You've had your break! Now get back to work. Bills need paying and your larder's empty."

As I turned into Cameron Street the first person I meet is the one and only Ged Howley. "Eamon how ya doin' cocker? Come and have a look at this trout I caught yesterday at Bridlington." I followed Ged up his stairs and into his bathroom. Well! I've seen some trout in my time, even tickled a couple. But this was something else. It's tail was as near as damn touching one end of the bath and its nose was over the plughole. "Ged, that's no trout." "Trust me it is." "What bait did you use, a dolphin?" I asked. "Ged from now on I'll believe any fish tale you tell me. Catch you later."

My customers on any Elton Fold round were lovely folk. Most days I'd be a little late getting done but if someone wanted a chat, well so be it, I wouldn't deny them. Some of the older folk I'd see had no visitors from one week to another. You can make their day just by acknowledging their existence. Not hard, is it? I call on George's Butchers. George has no fewer than a hundred small mincing machines hanging from the ceiling of his Ainsworth Road shop. The week before my hospital stay he'd taken on a young Irish lad by the name of Shaun, he was to work side by side with George's other helper, Michelle. "Hi George! Where's the young fella?" "Ouch I had to sack him." "You're joking, why?" "Left him on his own last Wednesday and he spent all day hanging the mince up." That's the joke out of the way George! I'll have a brew now.

Eventually I reached the home of the Hamer family on Holcombe Avenue. Russ, Kath and their two daughters had been having mailbags left in their garage for around 25 years. Kath's maiden name was Forrest. She's the sister of John Forrest, the former Bury FC 'keeper nicknamed 'Jungle', why, I'd no idea. I was acquainted with most of the Forest family. Three of the sons spent time between the sticks. I'd played alongside Mick for The Thrush and Greg with Elton Fold, both cracking keepers. The thing with the Forrests was they were all as strong as oxes, seems fitting they came from farming stock. They began their lives at Green Farm, Walshaw.

Greg was the one I knew best, spending a couple of seasons playing together for the Fold. He was one amazing lad who knew no fear. The truth being, if not for Greg's heroics in goal there's no way we'd have stayed in the top half of the league. Greg, for a living, was delivering coal. Every now and then I'd see his wagon pull up in the distance and more often than not watch as Greg made his way humping two huge sacks of coal one over each shoulder. Recently I was chatting to a mutual friend Robin Lomax. Robin was reminiscing about one particular night him and Greg visited a handful of the pubs round Elton, 'The Klondyke', 'The Woolpack' when Frank McDougal, the ex Aberdeen striker was the landlord, 'Elton Lib' then on to 'The Dusty Miller' finished at the 'Help Me Thro'. According to Robin's calculations Greg had supped 25 pints of bitter followed by a back street pee that went on for ten minutes.

Sadly Greg passed on a couple of years back. The turnout was fitting for one of our own. Another well-loved Bury lad lost to us much too soon. As they would be working it would be Saturday when Russ and Kath were at home. Russ would make a brew and then the three of us would have a chat. The Hamer family are staunch Bury fans so we had plenty to discuss. Being a Bury fan is similar albeit on a smaller scale, to being a City fan. Frustrating as hell but at the end of the day they're our home team and as such have our unwavering support. Wouldn't it be lovely if all the City, United, Liverpool etc. Bury-born supporters all decided to support their home team. Imagine! The gates would be huge, forcing ground improvements. We'd be in a position to strengthen our squad. Before we knew where we were we'd be in the Premiership. Think on you wayward supporters. Alright! I know I support my old amateur club but if for any reason I stopped, you'd find me at Gigg Lane. All these things discussed in the comfort of their kitchen. Isn't it lovely spending time with like minded people. I love it.

Time to move on. Before I finish my round, if I've time, I call on Marjory, a sprightly lady in her '80s. Older folk have a calming effect on me. And I take time out to pick their brains. If you've lived so long without any mental problems well there's not much you haven't learned. The elders of society are owners of a wealth of mostly untapped knowledge, I make the most of them. Marjorie was at her door as I was passing. "Kettle's on." "OK Marj, be in in a minute." After finishing the rest of Birkdale Drive I entered Marjorie's living room. "Before you have your brew Eamon could you do something for me?" "What's that Marj?" "My neck's seized up. I've some olive oil, could you massage it in?" "Err. Err. Right Marj!" Marjorie then lifted her top up to her shoulders.. She then bent over her table slap in the middle of her huge bay window. Hesitantly I took my position behind her and proceeded to massage her neck, never opening my eyes once, unable to accept the scene from out in the street. What a way to finish my first day back.

Friday's at Big Jims

Religiously every Friday afternoon after work me and half a dozen others would make our way to 'Big Jims'. A large open plan café situated at the centre of the indoor market. One of the lads, John Szepufi or 'Zeppy' was, for me, an inspirational lad. On the rare occasions I got the blues I invariably thought of John. I wasn't down for long after.

At the age of 16 John contracted a muscle-wasting disease. Over the following years his condition deteriorated to the point where his days now begin thus: at 7am each workday a care worker arrives to help John get out of bed. This is achieved with the help of a hoist. After a struggle John is sitting in his wheelchair placed at the side of his bed. A specially fitted lift transfers John from his bedroom to his living room, after a quick breakfast he's out the door, operating the electric ramp that lowers him and his chair to street level. The waiting mini bus conveys John to his place of work, Remploy's new mill at Pilsworth Industrial Estate. After the eight hours work John will make his way back to his Chesham home. I've known John for around ten years now and never once in that time have I heard him moan about his lot. In fact he's always sending himself up.

Once I made the mistake of telling him to give his job up. I was told in no uncertain terms to go away in short jerky movements. "I'll earn my own money thanks very much." That's me told. On the occasions John deems fit to bless us with his presence on a night out you couldn't get the bugger off the dance floor. At the café John is never slow to give his opinion on every topic discussed. Along with Sacko, Kenny and whoever, things are never dull. So yes, if I ever start feeling sorry for myself, well I just think of John.

Old and Lonely

I know I go on a lot about the old folk but after joining the Royal Mail as a postie it was probably the sad realisation of the sheer amount of lonely old folk out there, also the fact it wouldn't be too long before I myself would be among their ranks that made me think. The sadder thing still was the majority of these marginalised folk had family members who were only noticeable by their absence. There would always be excuses whispered, validating the absent loved ones. If this all sounds a bit harsh that's because I've witnessed this scenario too often to be detached. I sound like a moral snob. I don't mean to. I can be as ignorant as the next fella in ignoring other people's feelings.

My awakening came one day on Bury Market. I ran into an old team mate from way back. We'd been chatting for about fifteen minutes. It was then that four words were uttered that ripped into me as efficiently as a knife. "I exist as well." The words came from my old mate's teenage daughter, sat quietly in her wheelchair, literally between me and her dad. I'm not often lost for words but all I could do was stare at the offended girl. Her dad spoke next. "This is my daughter Clare." I mumbled something to the two of them and made my exit. I can't tell you how deeply this incident upset me. How thoughtless. Me. Who considered himself a decent thoughtful fella. How many times must I have done the same thing? That poor girl Clare, what must she think of me? I must have spent the rest of the day beating myself up for being such a thoughtless pig. I finally found some peace of mind, after making a promise to myself to never allow it to happen again.

That night after putting an old CD of the great country songwriter John Prine on, I climbed into the hot Radox bath I'd prepared. Have you ever noticed if the situation is just right, a song you've heard countless times before and you thought you knew like an old friend, then one day for one reason or another, maybe you're senses happen to be heightened, whatever; you listen and hear it properly for the first time. There were a few lines in one of the songs that maybe because of what had gone on earlier in the day had a profound effect on me. John was singing about the old folk, the invisible old folk:

"So if you're walking down the street sometime
And spot some hollow ancient eyes
Please don't pass 'em by and stare
As if you didn't care
Say hello in there
Hello"

So, another promise to myself, to get more proactive with the old folk.

The next morning I had the chance to put it into practice. Walking along Newbold Street approaching me was an old dear I'd passed many times. I'd never seen her with anyone or for that matter talk to anyone. Well today will be different because I'll make it different. Putting my bag down and standing in her path, we were practically toe to toe before she was even aware I was there. Cupping her face with one hand I said "you look lovely today darling" then kissed her on the cheek, picked up my bag and said "I'll see you soon." I know this was a little radical, I think I had a bit of the devil in me. If nothing else I'd given that lady something to keep her mind occupied for a while. Now if I'm honest I had no idea how she would react and in truth I didn't hang around to find out.

A couple of days later, same street, same lady, as we passed I said "morning gorgeous." Now she didn't answer me but the sweet smile that lit up her face was priceless. So now no old folk pass me without a polite greeting, sometimes its left one sided but that's rare, some actually look visibly shocked that someone's acknowledged their existence. I realise there's a lot of happy contented old folk, it's just there's also a lot of very lonely old folk and they don't go round with signs, so it's best to adopt blanket coverage.

An Oversight

After completing my humble efforts of recording my recollections of life growing up in Bury and tales from its amateur football scene, I confess to a nagging feeling of maybe missing something. Well actually lots of things. I suppose it is always thus. Things will come to mind, people remind you of things. I decided to let most of it slide for now but something my mate Paul Lomax told me just wouldn't leave me be. "Eamon you've only paid passing reference to Highfield Utd. I advise you to pay their old manager, John Flynn, a visit." Eventually I though "What is the harm".

I was aware Highfield were a good side. Damn I had even played against them for my old club Abbey Hey. There were good but not that good. The last game I played against them we had beat them at their place 1–3. I remember the game mainly for one incident – picking the ball up on the right flank I pushed the ball past Joe Murty. Next thing I am yanked back by the collar of my shirt. I played the rest of the game with a perfectly intact collar and my shirt clinging to it by a few threads. Anyway, armed with John's Springside Road address, supplied by the man himself, I set off on my trusty bicycle speedily towards Bury Bridge.

The light was fading as I freewheeled down Springside Road, checking the numbers as I passed. At last I pulled up at the door of John's lovely home. Answering my knock

Highfield United, arguably the finest team of their time.

at his door John's beaming face and strong handshake put me at my ease. Realising this would be the first conversation I have had with John, after 20 minutes in his company all I could think was what a smashing bloke. After an hour of exchanging views on life in general we came to the reason for my visit. John, without saying another word, left the dining table we were sat at. He returned shortly and along with the words "There you go" placed in front of me a large photo of the 1980–81 Manchester Premier League winning Highfield side. Looking at the lads gathered for that photo I was completely dumbstruck. It was a while before I gathered myself enough to mutter "What a team!". I said to John "If me and a couple of muckers sat down and between us picked what we considered Bury's finest squad this would probably be it". This team had it all. Built on a solid defence with the likes of Martin Howard, Steve Woods, the late great Greg Forrest and midfield including the classy George Bennett, Titch Heaton and Pete Beaument; a forward line boasting my personal favourite Dave Wolfenden, Paul Dickinson and Alan Whitmore. Any of these lads would be a dream addition to any of the local sides. I think the best compliment I could pay John and his former charges would be to say I would have willingly paid money to have watched this outfit.

Pride in All

It is easy to assume when cups and trophies are won in amateur circles that the glory is restricted to that particular club at that particular time. In truth it reverberates around this football loving town, shared by lads such as myself who take real pride in the successes of our local teams. We love nothing more than being sat round at some social gathering discussing amateur football past and present. The joy of listening to lads whose opinions you respect. Many is the time I have had my own opinion changed by someone with greater insight into the subject being discussed.

When certain players, teams or managers are mentioned there is a definite sense of pride. This pride isn't restricted to successful sides; as an example one of only half a dozen local senior sides still playing competitive football is Hargreaves FC. Managed by Ian Chesters and his sidekick Paul Kliyz, you would have to walk a few country miles to find two nicer blokes. For the last 25 years Ian and Paul, week in and week out, do what is needed to get 11 lads out on that pitch come Saturday and if that means donning a kit themselves so be it. While Hargreaves trophy cabinet hasn't ever been straining with silverware, well so what. These lads are just content to be playing the beautiful game. Some of my favourite games and seasons ended with no trophies. Not everyone can be winners. God bless the lads who are just happy to be there.

Other stalwarts include Charlie Cooper of Chesham Fold fame. Never got to know Charlie but if his lads Jimmy and Peter are anything to go by, he must have been some bloke. Pete Lockey of Fishpool FC was a great advert for the game. I am proud to include my brother Pat and his sidekick Les Barlow among them. These two spent every Sunday morning of the season, rain or shine, rounding up their troops. On away games we were to meet outside Iceland on Rochdale Road. Among our ranks were some real characters who were proud to represent Peel FC. Their love of the game only matched by their love of the womenfolk.

Now these lads played Saturday as well as Sunday. Saturday was widely accepted as the football Sabbath. As a result some of the lads either stayed home Friday nights or if they ventured out they took it easy. Come Saturday night, well that is different. They weren't about to give up both nights. Young fit lads, most of whom had given up their Friday nights they were out to enjoy themselves. As a result come Sunday morning occasionally we found ourselves a player or players down. They had had a great night and woke to find themselves in a strange bed and sometimes in a strange town. An intoxicated body clock amazingly still functioning would attempt to mobilise its host. In a dreamlike state they would detach themselves from the bed and its occupant, fall to their knees fumbling for their clothes in the dark. More than once lads have turned

The Raven FC – a who's who of Bury's finest

up for the game in very fetching underwear, mumbling an apologetic farewell to the bemused lass, the poor girl not knowing quite the reason for the rushed exit. In those days this scenario would be played out all over town. Guys like out Pat and Les stuck doggedly to their task of rallying the troops. Eventually the shout would go up "Right lets get off" and we would be on our way.

Faith

I still consider myself a Christian as a lot of the Christian doctrine I admire very much but for me there's something missing. No longer being a practicing Catholic has left me in a bit of a spiritual void. Attempting to fill this void I made a personal pact with a supposed deity to go through life attempting not to harm anyone in any way and where I can, to help folk along the way. And if that means being condemned to eternal damnation then so be it.

During the time I was in Nashville with my brother Michael on our pilgrimage to the mecca of country music, we couldn't help but notice the sheer number of Baptist churches, practically one on every corner. One sunny afternoon while passing one of the aforementioned, our feet involuntarily led us to the front doors of a lovely modern Baptist church. The joyous singing and clapping coming from within was so infectious we couldn't help ourselves from creeping closer, trying to get a glimpse of the very happy sounding congregation. With our faces pressed up to the glass door a very large gentleman approached the door. My initial instinct was to exit the scene. Our Michael's hand on my shoulder relaxed me. The giant opened the door and in a voice entrenched in the deep south he drawled "what can I do for you gentlemen?" As my throat had seized up our Michael answered. We were just enjoying the singing. We were greeted with a loud "Oh, you're English. Well fellas why don't you both come in, you're more than welcome." Me and our kid were dropped on, we just stared at the friendly giant. After some more coaxing we found ourselves stood at the back of a palatial room. I reckon there wasn't a man, woman or child who didn't look round to check out the two pale-faced intruders. We didn't know what to do or say, if anything.

We both managed a pathetic semi-wave where our arms barely passed our waists. God please stop looking at us. Our giant friend whispering something to what I assumed was the preacher, whereupon he addressed the congregation and asked them to welcome our guests from little old England. We were then treated to a lovely chorus of 'Welcome Friends'. I felt such a mixture of emotions, I looked at Michael and he couldn't conceal his enjoyment , smiling like a Cheshire cat. I was relieved when the preacher led the congregation in a song both me and our kid were familiar with. 'I Saw The Light' a song I happen to love, sung to me by Johnny Cash and the Carter family. So it felt so good to be able to join in with the lovely singing of the folk around us. And there was no doubt about it, me and our kid got caught up in the joyous atmosphere and it was beyond us to stop ourselves thrusting our arms in the air and doing a sort of dance. Yes, dancing, can you believe that, in a church? Finally the preacher, a handsome silver-haired man of around 60 gave his sermon with both passion and conviction and very animatedly. After thanking and hugging what seemed a hundred new friends me and our kid finally left a church feeling elated.

Marriage Beckons

Sometimes on Fridays I'd get down to 'Big Jims' early. Round the back of the café were four stools, above which was a narrow shelf for cups of tea or coffee. It was here I waited for the others. Opposite this area was a clothes stall, on this clothes stall worked a lovely lady called Dawn. If Dawn wasn't busy and she had time we'd have a brew together. I left it a while before I asked her out. Me and Sue had parted company amicably a couple of months before. For our first date we went to Pic's Bar on Market Street. We both enjoyed ourselves. Around three months later we were both in my kitchen enjoying a couple of good bottles of wine, listening to some lovely Irish songs. I was shocked to find Dawn knew all the words, even correcting me on occasions. I know it sounds corny but I was blown away. To have a companion to sing and drink good wine with and enjoy both as much as myself felt so good. So after a year of enjoying each other's company we decided we loved each other enough to join ourselves in matrimony. I know what you are thinking – third marriage – what can I say? Doesn't sound good does it. I won't try to justify myself only to say I enjoy good relationships with both my ex-wives and our priority will always remain our kids. Well we had a lovely day and in Dawn's son Shane, daughter Tanya, their partners and children, I've acquired some lovely folk to go through life with.

Recently, because of health issues, my days as a postie have come to an end. I miss the camaraderie with my work colleagues but not getting up at daft o' clock. We've recently acquired a computer which I've no idea how to operate. Luckily Dawn has no such problem, so she keeps me in contact with friends in far off lands. Bury continues to attempt to improve itself and for the most part it does, the Rock project being the latest scheme. Any visitor to Bury couldn't help but be impressed by our fine, not-so-little town. The efforts by the folk connected with Bury in Bloom should give themselves a pat on the back. From the flower beds at the Barracks on Bolton Road, the figurines leading up to Bolton Street to the town centre baskets, a real treat for the eye. It's so good to walk round Bury bumping into friends new and old with time to catch up. An occasional night out in a town with everything you'd want. Great pubs and spoilt for places to dine and finish off in the best pub in town "The White Lion" packed every weekend with young and mature folk, having the craic with Billy Stanley belting out songs of yesteryear.

Get-togethers are held at mine or our Michael's home with all the old crowd round. The Kavanagh's love these get-togethers. It's a time to touch base with a collection of lovable lunatics who enrich our lives just by being themselves. On more than one occasion when on the subject of our younger generation we consider ourselves in a position now, rightly or wrongly, where we can have a valid opinion on the matter. We all agree some of the things we got up to might be a hindrance to our passage through the pearly gates. One difference that stands out for all of us is the subject of respect. At the time of our youth even the kids reckoned to be beyond the pale, held a grudging respect for their elders and women folk. Today if you witness a youth showing respect in any given situation it's a real talking point, it's so rare. Walking the streets in the late evenings without doubt retains a sense of unease. I don't pretend to know the reasons or the answers to today's problems but respect and common decency are the qualities that make life worth living. Never before have these mainstays of a free society been in such short supply.

Those of us lucky enough to enjoy the company of many decent minded family and friends tend to seek each other's company more and more. One of the reasons for this is to keep each other grounded and sane, in a world that frankly is losing its way. You try to stay optimistic. One thing we all agree on is that we were born into the luckiest generation that ever lived. Happy childhoods in which we could roam over hill and dale without a care. Never had to take up arms against another human being. And, in the main, spent all our adult life in gainful employment and regular reunions to chat about old times and sing some old tunes. Sadly I find it hard to imagine another generation being so lucky. We can only hope.

Over the Water

I'm writing this as I sit in my comfortable upholstered seat on the huge Stenna Express docked at Holyhead in the company of my wife Dawn and son Lee. The long journey down was almost enjoyable. As we sit here we are surrounded by all the comforts and all the requirements to ensure an enjoyable passage. As Lee and Dawn relax into a much needed nap, my mind drifts back to my first trip across the water with Mum and Dad and my seven siblings as detailed elsewhere. That was the 60s.

This trip, as many others to Ireland, would see me visit Dad's birthplace of Avoca in County Wicklow, a gorgeous little village made famous by the TV series 'Ballykissangel'. With the television crews now long gone the place has returned to its original tranquil self, the only reminder being that the Fountain Pub has maintained its fictional TV name of Fitzgeralds, and a novelty shop. Dad's old home has been greatly improved by a builder by the name of Mike Duffy who bought it some years ago. Mike and his lovely wife showed typical Irish hospitality in inviting a gang of us into their home a few years back. After they insisted we take tea with them we were shown pictures of the original building, up to then my son Lee had never seen it. I always came away from the house feeling really emotional.

Dad's birthplace, No.1 Beach Road, Avoca, County Wicklow, EIRE. It looks idyllic, but life was hard for Dad and his siblings.

I looked searchingly round the surrounding countryside, knowing Dad as a boy would have trod every nook and cranny. In summer he would have been barefoot. God I wish I could peep into those times, a momentary presence, watching Dad play, talk, how he interacted with others. I know practically nothing about him. Wish so much I'd questioned him when I had the chance. By contrast Mum was an open book and the best read a son could hope for. As in the times before, our trip would end with a proper Irish night in. This includes a great chat, lovely food and finally someone, usually cousin John, playing the guitar while we all sang a song one of us has excitedly suggested. Entwined with lovely poems and tales I absolutely love. To me the Irish brogue is music in itself.

The Kavanagh Clan

Growing up with my siblings amongst other things was never boring. Each one with their own particular character and quirks. Michael, the baby of the family, was to endure years of snide, cruel jibes from yours truly. I know. Pathetic or what? Thankfully we've ended up close. Kathleen, my younger sister by 13 months is lovely but you don't cross her.

Next comes our Margaret, Mags, three years older than me but if anything a bit dafter. Mags loved a giggle and had a very contagious laugh; no matter how hard she tried to be good, the devil on her shoulder sometimes got the better of her. Next is my older brother John. From being a kiddie, trouble would always find him or he'd seek it out, never malicious or cruel, I suppose just naughty. One incident sticks in my mind concerning John. On our visit to our grandparents in Ireland in the '60s, they had an ancient water barrel outside their front door. It was for washing their clothes. Technology was a far off addition to life for these simple folk.   Well, one morning while out exploring, John came upon a rusty old iron fence rail. To John's young mind this was a spear and he became a young native, perfecting his hunting skills. And the old water barrel wasn't a water barrel. No! As John attempted to explain after Grandma's screams had brought us all to view the cause of the commotion, we were greeted with the sight of Grandma breaking her heart crying, staring at the water barrel with two thirds of the fence rail hanging from its side, the last third embedded through its middle along with a trail of water pouring to the ground, forming a fair sized pool. An ashen-faced John looked bewildered at all the commotion, after all it was just an old barrel.

John's diet of chips with anything as long as it wasn't healthy would come to haunt him in the future. Mum really tried to get him to eat more healthily but in the end even she gave up. When you're cooking for ten a varied menu is a big ask. Then comes my older sister Sheila. She who must be obeyed. As you've probably guessed Sheila was a very strong character and ruled us kids with a rod of steel. She had a way with her which compelled you to obey her. Of course she enjoyed her power. One day when we were a little older, my patience snapped and I ended up fighting with Sheila. Afterwards she was crying, which cut me to the quick. How could I? I can honestly say that day I hurt myself a lot more than I hurt our She!

Later in life our Sheila would be employed as Sister at Pendlebury Hospital. Perfect. Then there's our Patrick, my older brother whose enthusiasm for the beautiful game set me on a long but mostly enjoyable path taking in so many clubs I've lost count. As a young man I often passed Pat's bedroom and heard Pat practicing on one of his many guitars. Music and football would always be the great loves of his life. The only music played in our house while Pat was present was country or Irish. Pat also enjoyed a drink, especially within the walls of what would be our local for some 25 years, The Peel Hotel on Rochdale Road.

Pat was very opinionated, to the extent that quite often it fetched him trouble. One night I walked into The Peel to find our Pat flat out on the floor, just coming round. Next to the vacant bar stool which moments earlier Pat occupied was Trevor Duckworth. Now Trevor wasn't a tall man but he was built like a Staffordshire Bull Terrier and looked just as mean. It was deceiving as he was a smashing bloke. As I knelt by our Pat to help him up, Denis the landlord says "Eamon before you start, your Pat was the instigator." As our Pat slowly came back to us, the three of us sat at the bar and enjoyed a good chat which ended with Pat and Trevor shaking hands. Pat would find himself involved in a couple more such incidents over the years till one St. Patrick's Day, after a good drink and a jig at the end of the night, Pat turned round and said. "Well that's it for me. No more beer!" Well the rest of the family took it with a pinch of salt but that was 13 years ago and not a drop has passed his lips, even after being tempted by well meaning family members. The thing about our Pat is that no matter what subject you raise with him, he'll have an opinion and some knowledge of it. He is honestly the most knowledgeable lad I've ever known.

Then there's the matriarch, our Mary who never tires at family get-togethers of telling the tale about being pushed around London in an orange box during the Blitz. And we never tire of hearing it? She is always guest of honour at our get-togethers. As a young woman she was stunning, I honestly believe Mary was never aware of her beauty, certainly she never played on it. There was no shortage of suitors beating a path to our door. Mary's gift lies in the way she makes anyone and everyone feel comfortable, any stranger could be left in a room with Mary no matter how shy they were they would soon fall into comfortable conversation with Mary and claiming her for their own.

A Regular Day in the Kavanagh Home

There's good and bad about belonging to a large family like ours, more good than bad. From our time on Dicky Bird Estate till well into our time in Oxford Street certain things were constant. Dad's routine of grafting all week then drinking himself into a stupor at weekends, Mum working regular nights at Robinson Kay home and keeping our home shipshape, Patrick following Dad's lead but where Dad would come home and head straight for the kitchen, emerging 15 minutes later with a couple of lamb chops on a plate, laughing because in his drunken state Dad mostly forgot to light the cooker. The chops would be devoured anyway. Patrick went straight to bed.

Mary was married by this time and Sheila was in a relationship. The rest of us were rarely in the house if the weather was fine. Round the Pimhole area there was plenty to do. Plenty of kids around, footy at Rocky Road park, tennis, bowls, crazy golf. Fun down by the river Roach or walking the streets, playing music of the day on our portable record players. So it tended to be around 8pm on school days when we all got together in front of the lovely fire Dad had built up. He would then enter the kitchen and come out a while later with a giant plate of toasted cheese and mugs of tea all round. The toast would be cut into fingers and slices of cheese to match. The butter was spread on the toast good and thick. I'd need a full page to explain how good it was. Strange how things stay with you. I maintained this practice with my own kids.

While in Oxford Street once you reached 14 years of age, you could stay up until 9.30pm. This made you feel so grown up. There were many dramas played out in that big old house but, even during the rough times, as soon as you crossed the threshold - and I know it's an overused word - but the sense of welcoming love was tangible. I didn't at the time but everyday now I feel so lucky to be a Kavanagh raised in a smashing town like Bury. As I write these last few words, we're approaching Remembrance Sunday. Health permitting, I will never miss this acknowledgment of our brave soldiers down the generations. Bury, being the home of the famous Lancashire Fusilier's, just makes it that bit more potent. God bless them all!

Printed in Great Britain
by Amazon